ACUTE
ANTERIOR

POLIOMYELITIS

(A COMMUNICABLE DISEASE)

Keep Out of this House

By Order of BOARD OF HEALTH

HEALTH OFFICER

H. M. Alexander Ptg. Co.
88 First St., S. F.

EPIDEMIC!

THE BATTLE AGAINST POLIO

by STEPHANIE TRUE PETERS

BENCHMARK BOOKS

MARSHALL CAVENDISH
NEW YORK

ACKNOWLEDGMENTS

With thanks to Allison Kavey, Lecturer, Department of the History of Science, Medicine, and Technology, Johns Hopkins University, Baltimore, for her careful reading of the manuscript.

Benchmark Books
Marshall Cavendish
99 White Plains Road
Tarrytown, New York 10591-9001
www.marshallcavendish.com

Book design by Michael Nelson

LIBRARY OF CONGRESS CATALOGING-IN-PUBLICATION DATA
Peters, Stephanie True, 1965-
The battle against polio / by Stephanie True Peters.
p. cm. — (Epidemic!)
Includes bibliographical references and index.
ISBN 0-7614-1635-8
1. Poliomyelitis—History—Juvenile literature.
I. Title II. Series: Peters, Stephanie True, 1965- . Epidemic!.
RC180.9.P48 2005
614.549—dc22
2004003408

Picture Research by Linda Sykes Picture Research, Inc., Hilton Head, S. C.

Photo credits: Front cover,14, 17, 20, 23, 24 (top), 24 (bottom), 25, 26, 56, 57: Bettmann/Corbis; ii, 30, 31: FDR Library, Hyde Park, NY; i, 9: National Library of Medicine; vii, 37: March of Dimes Birth Defects Foundation; vii: ML Suckley/FDR Library/AP/Wide World Photos; x: National Archives of Canada; 3: Aventis Pasteur, Canada; 5: Hospital for Sick Children Archives, Toronto; 6: Custom Medical Stock; 8: Ny Carlsberg Glypothek, Copenhagen, Denmark; 11:Museum of the City of New York; 12: Corbis; 16: Roosevelt Warm Springs Institute for Rehabilitation, Warm Springs, GA; 19: Al Fenn/Time Life Pictures/Getty Images; 25(top), 27: Naomi Rogers, Dirt and Disease, Polio Before FDR, Rutgers U Press; pages 37, 65; 34: Hulton Deutsch/Corbis; 39: Hulton Archive/Getty Images; 41: Private Collection; 42, 51, 54, 60: AP/Wide World Photos; 47: Time Life Pictures/Getty Images; 52: Getty Images; 55:"Polio Canada". Polio Canada is a new national polio survivors network that is administered by the Ontario March of Dimes (http://www.poliocanada.com; back cover: Bill Bridges/Time Life Pictures/Getty Images

PRINTED IN CHINA
1 3 5 6 4 2

Front cover: A photograph taken during the 1916 New York City epidemic

Back cover: A drive-up polio vaccine clinic, September 1960

Half title: Polio quarantine notice, San Francisco, early 1900s

Title page: The First Birthday Ball at Warm Springs, Georgia, 1934

From the Author, page vii: A group of Polio Pioneers, 1954

CONTENTS

FROM THE AUTHOR · vii

INTRODUCTION
TRAGEDY AND TRIUMPH · ix

CHAPTER ONE
FROM OBSCURITY TO EPIDEMIC · 1
WHAT IS POLIO? · 2
POLIO'S EARLY HISTORY · 8
ON THE HEELS OF THE INDUSTRIAL REVOLUTION · 10

CHAPTER TWO
THE EARLY YEARS OF POLIO RESEARCH · 13
DR. IVAR WICKMAN · 15
LANDSTEINER AND POPPER · 17
DR. SIMON FLEXNER · 19

CHAPTER THREE
POLIO ON THE RISE · 22
NEW YORK CITY EPIDEMIC, 1916 · 23
FRANKLIN DELANO ROOSEVELT · 28
A BRIGHT SPOT · 33

CHAPTER FOUR
COPING WITH THE INCURABLE · 35
THE IRON LUNG · 37
SISTER KENNY, CRUSADER AGAINST POLIO · 38
ORDINARY PEOPLE, EXTRAORDINARY LIVES · 41

CHAPTER FIVE
VACCINE TRIALS—AND ERRORS   44
BRODIE AND KOLMER   45
THE TYPING PROGRAM   48
THE 1952 EPIDEMIC   49

CHAPTER SIX
SALK AND SABIN   53
THE SABIN VACCINE   56

CONCLUSION
POLIO TODAY   59

TIME LINE OF POLIO EVENTS   61
GLOSSARY   62
TO FIND OUT MORE   63
BIBLIOGRAPHY   65
NOTES ON QUOTATIONS   66
INDEX   68

FROM THE AUTHOR

The idea for a series of books about epidemics came to me while I was sitting in the doctor's office with my son. He had had a sleepless, feverish night. I suspected he had an ear infection and looked forward to the doctor confirming my diagnosis and prescribing antibiotics.

While waiting for the doctor to appear, I suddenly realized that the situation I was in—a mother looking to relieve her child's pain—was hardly new. Humans have had an ongoing battle against disease throughout history. Today, we have tremendous knowledge of how the human body works. We understand how viruses and bacteria attack and how the body defends itself. Through immunizations and simple hygiene, we're often able to prevent disease in the first place. Our ancestors were not so knowledgeable, nor so lucky.

In this series, I have tried to put a human face on five epidemics that laid millions low. All five occurred in the past and have since been medically controlled. Yet in some areas of the world, similar stories are still being played out today as humans struggle against such enemies as AIDS, Ebola virus, hantavirus, and other highly contagious diseases. In the fight against disease, we may never have the upper hand. Microscopic foes are hard to fight.

One of only two known photographs of President Franklin D. Roosevelt in his wheelchair.

Roosevelt was polio's most famous victim—and its strongest opponent.

TRAGEDY AND TRIUMPH

The history of polio is one of tragedy and triumph. At the height of the worst epidemics—in the first part of the twentieth century—the disease infected, crippled, and killed thousands. It struck terror into the hearts of parents. Would their child escape infection—or become one of the many who were permanently crippled, forced to wear leg braces, use crutches or a wheelchair, or live out the rest of his or her life encased in the breathing apparatus known as the iron lung?

At first, no one knew what caused the disease. Even when doctors began to gain some understanding, they remained baffled for decades as to how the illness was transmitted. Each summer of the first half of the twentieth century saw more and more victims of a disease that a century earlier did not even have an official name. Yet as the incidence of polio increased, so did the number of people dedicated to fighting it. Their successes built upon one another until at last a means of prevention was discovered—and polio was brought under control.

The war against polio continues, for the disease still stalks parts of the world. But the final battle is within sight, as people across the globe unite to make this old crippler truly a thing of the past.

This book explores the history of polio, tracking its emergence from an obscure disease to one known and feared worldwide. It examines the efforts of the men and women who pioneered polio research, treatment, and prevention. And finally, it reports the triumphs in the global fight against this crippling disease.

CHAPTER ONE

FROM OBSCURITY TO EPIDEMIC

I WOKE UP AND TRIED TO GET OUT OF BED BUT FELL TO THE FLOOR
BECAUSE MY LEGS WOULD NO LONGER MOVE ME, AND I WAS RATHER LIMP.
I WAS THEN TAKEN TO THE UNIVERSITY HOSPITAL IN INDIANAPOLIS
WHERE I WAS DIAGNOSED WITH POLIO.

—Richard O., 1940

n a certain Friday morning in September 1949, when future children's book author Peg Schulze (now Kehret) was twelve, she started to feel strange. She wasn't thinking, at the time, about the polio epidemic sweeping the United States. She was looking forward wholeheartedly to her school's homecoming parade later that day. Then, in the middle of Chorus, her left leg started to twitch. On her way back to her locker after rehearsal, her legs gave way entirely, and she collapsed. Worried friends helped her up. Somehow, she managed to walk the twelve blocks home for lunch.

Peg knew she was sick, but she didn't want to miss the parade. She tried to hide her illness from her mother. But Peg's temper-

Opposite:

A two-and-a-half-year-old boy struggles to take steps after surviving a polio epidemic in the early 1950s.

1

ature rapidly spiked to 102 degrees. Her neck, back, and legs began to ache; a weariness like nothing she'd ever felt came over her. That afternoon, Peg slept through the parade, too sick even to care.

Peg and her parents thought she had the flu. They were wrong. The following morning, her doctor diagnosed her with poliomyelitis.

Peg's life literally changed overnight. One day she could walk, run, and hold her own books. The next, she was paralyzed from the neck down, unable to move her arms or legs. Peg spent the next year of her life struggling to regain mobility. After months of intense physical therapy, she succeeded. Not every poliomyelitis victim was as fortunate.

WHAT IS POLIO?

Poliomyelitis, or polio as it is more commonly known, is a terrifying disease that struck in epidemic proportions from the late 1800s to the mid-1900s. It left thousands dead, paralyzed, or with atrophied limbs that created lifelong disability. The disease usually attacked children, although adults could be victims too. As parents tried to cope with polio's threat, researchers worked feverishly to discover its cause, develop a cure, and stop it from spreading. But until the disease was fully understood, no one could cure it, or stop it.

Today we know that polio is caused by a virus. A virus is a submicroscopic agent made up of a protective shell of proteins surrounding the virus's genetic material. Viruses are parasitic, meaning they cannot reproduce without a host body. A virus typically enters a host body through the nose or mouth, when the host inhales or ingests material contaminated with the virus.

Once the virus has successfully entered a body, it seeks out cells to help it reproduce. When it finds an appropriate cell, the virus attaches itself to the cell membrane. Then the virus's protective shell makes a hole in the membrane through which the virus injects its genetic material. Once inside, the genetic material takes over the cell and forces it to make

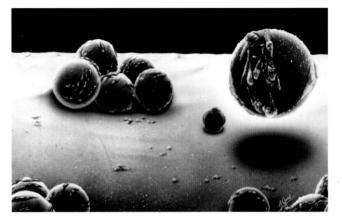

This painting, made from a photograph of a microscope image, shows cells (spheres) infected with the poliovirus (droplets).

copies of the virus. The cell bursts when it can no longer contain all the copies, showering nearby cells with the virus—and the process begins again.

People usually become infected with polio when they drink contaminated water. Polio is a waterborne disease. It is most often transmitted from person to person via water contaminated with virus-laden fecal matter. People can become infected if they swim in water containing the virus or if they drink contaminated water. Contact with an infected person, or with food that has been touched by contaminated water or an infected person, can also spread the disease.

Poliovirus enters the body orally, through the mouth, and leaves the body in fecal matter. Once in the body, it multiplies in the cells of the throat and intestines. The first signs of infection appear between four to fourteen days after exposure to the virus. Those first signs can be severe.

"I was sitting on the potty screaming my lungs out," wrote James Gary Brown, who remembers coming down with polio at age three. "My stomach hurt and my head felt like it was being crushed. I was naked and must have had a high fever for I was freezing and sweating at the same time."

Not all reactions to poliovirus need be so intense, however.

In fact, for doctors facing the epidemic conditions of the last century, one of the trickiest parts of fighting polio was recognizing it. That's because most people who catch polio feel as if they just have a cold; some may not even notice it. A few feel as though they've come down with a stomach virus. Surprisingly, in fewer than 2 percent of cases does the well-known and sometimes deadly paralysis take hold.

Polio was named for that small percentage of cases that end in paralysis. The word *poliomyelitis* comes from the Greek words *polios,* which means "gray," and *myelos,* which means "marrow." Marrow here does not refer to the stuff inside bones, but to the spinal cord found within the hollow of the spinal column. This spinal cord is one main part of the central nervous system, which controls the body's muscles. The other part of the central nervous system is the brain. The two parts together are commonly called "gray matter." In severe cases of polio, the virus spreads from the throat and intestines and attacks the gray matter. Another name for poliomyelitis is infantile paralysis. It earned this name because 80 to 90 percent of polio cases occur in children under the age of three.

After doctors realized that not all polio cases result in paralysis, they learned that polio manifests, or shows, itself in four different ways: inapparent, abortive, non-paralytic, and paralytic. Inapparent polio is the mildest, with fatigue, headache, sore throat, and fever as the chief symptoms. Abortive polio shares these symptoms, but also includes vomiting, abdominal pain and constipation, or, occasionally, diarrhea. Victims of non-paralytic polio may have all or some of these symptoms as well as stiff necks and achy, sore limbs. The most severe, rarest form of the disease is paralytic polio.

Paralytic polio occurs when the virus moves into the central nervous system and weakens or destroys motor neurons, the cells responsible for telling muscles how and when to move. In a healthy body, the brain sends messages through the spinal cord to the motor neurons, and the motor neurons pass the impulse to the muscles. When poliovirus attacks motor neurons, the messages from the brain don't get to the muscles, and they become paralyzed.

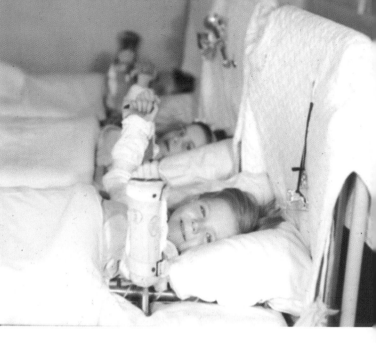

Some children afflicted with paralytic polio lost the use of their arms.

These muscles do not, however, lose feeling. The spinal cord also contains nerve cells that tell the body when it feels pain, changes in temperature, and other sensations. These cells are not affected by poliovirus, so although patients may not be able to move, they still have feeling in their paralyzed muscles.

Although every muscle in the body is vulnerable to poliovirus, the leg muscles are most often affected. In more severe cases, the trunk and arms also become paralyzed, leaving patients quadriplegic, unable to move from the neck down. A few paralyzed victims—about 5 to 10 percent—also suffer paralysis of the muscles that control breathing. Unless they are hooked up to a machine to help them breathe, they die.

Polio patients' chances of recovering from paralysis depend upon the amount of damage to their motor neurons. All paralytic polio patients suffer from atrophy (weakness from lack of use) in paralyzed muscles. When such paralysis strikes children, the atrophied limbs don't grow normally. Many young survivors are forced to use crutches, leg braces, or wheelchairs for the rest of their lives. Corrective surgery is often used as children with polio grow, to help them regain a normal range of movement. Some polio survivors can regain full mobility with proper care and time. In cases where only some of the neurons that control a muscle are dam-

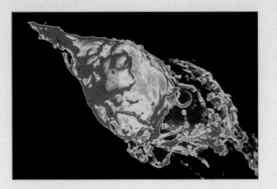

Poliovirus attacks a vulnerable cell.

A DISEASE OF MANY NAMES

The disease we call poliomyelitis has been known by many names throughout the centuries. In 1789, Dr. Michael Underwood called it a "debility of the lower extremities." Jacob von Heine named it "spinal infantile paralysis" in 1843. The word *poliomyelitis* was first used in 1872, by Adolph Kussmaul, who called the disease "poliomyelitis anterior acuta." *Anterior* referred to the fact that most damage occurred in the anterior horn—the part that contains motor neurons—of the spinal cord. *Acuta* simply meant acute, or severe.

In 1907, Dr. Ivar Wickman gave the disease the name "Heine-Medin," by which it was known for forty years. Then, in 1947, doctors reverted to an earlier name, shortening it to "poliomyelitis." The public shortened this name even further, to "polio." This is the name best known to most people.

Like all viruses, poliovirus mutates, or changes, over time. In 1949 polio was given three new names—for the three types of virus that scientists discovered. Type I is called Brunhilde, after a chimpanzee. Type I poliovirus was isolated in spinal cord tissue taken from this chimpanzee. Type II is called Lansing, after a town in Michigan. Lansing was the hometown of a man who died of polio. Samples taken of this man's brain and spinal cord contained Type II. Type III was obtained from an eleven-year-old boy from Los Angeles. This type is called Leon, after the boy.

Identifying the three viral types was crucial in the development of a polio vaccine because antibodies that fought against one strain did not defend against the other two. Therefore, the vaccine had to contain all three strains in order to be effective. Within five years of the positive identification of Brunhilde, Lansing, and Leon, the first effective vaccine against polio had been developed.

aged, the remaining healthy neurons learn to control the muscle by themselves. They even branch around impaired neurons to do their job. Only when the neuron damage is extensive or complete is the victim paralyzed for life.

Poliovirus symptoms are more likely to be severe in older children and adults. Infants and very young children often show no signs of infection at all. These young children with inapparent polio are a great danger to others, however, because they carry the virus and can spread it.

There are three types of poliovirus, known as Type I, Type II, and Type III. The immune system reacts the same way to all three types. How strongly it reacts determines whether the infection will be asymptomatic, mild, or severe.

The immune system's job is fighting infections; two of the system's major tools are a protein called interferon and white blood cells. When a virus invades a cell, the cell can't defend itself or resist the command to reproduce the virus. However, the cell can warn other cells that an attack is under way by creating interferon. Cells that sense interferon protect themselves by making an antiviral protein to shut out the virus, slowing its spread.

White blood cells also react to interferon and swing into action to defend the body from invasion. Some white blood cells make antibodies, agents that attach themselves to viruses and make it impossible for the viruses to enter cells. Viruses that can't enter cells can't replicate. They become vulnerable to attack and are eventually destroyed.

Because making antibodies takes time—as long as two weeks—people may feel sick while the immune system goes to work. After a particular virus is killed, however, the antibodies that attacked it remain in the body, ready to immediately repel future invasions by that virus. Antibody levels never decrease—in fact, they can increase if the person is exposed to the virus again. Thanks to these antibodies, the person has lifelong immunity to the virus. The poliovirus poses a special problem, however. An individual must be exposed to all three types before becoming completely immune.

Doctors can tell if someone has been exposed to a particular virus by analyzing a blood sample to see what antibodies it contains. For instance, if the blood contains antibodies to poliovirus Type I, doctors know that at one time the person was exposed to that particular virus.

It is possible for the body to create antibodies without actually suffering through an illness. Doctors have long used vaccines to "trick" the immune system into making antibodies. Vaccines contain either live, weakened viruses, or viruses that have been killed. When the vaccine enters the bloodstream, the immune system reacts by making antibodies—but only rarely does the person get sick. And the antibodies usually last a lifetime, just like those made in response to actual illness. Today, children generally get regular vaccinations against many diseases, including polio. Most of them grow up never knowing the maladies that once terrorized humanity.

POLIO'S EARLY HISTORY

Many medical historians believe polio existed at least as long ago as 1500 B.C. An ancient Egyptian stone carving depicts a young man with a withered leg leaning on a staff for support. The man's deformity looks as though it could have been caused by polio. Ancient Greeks described cases of paralysis that some historians think may have been polio.

Historians believe polio caused this ancient Egyptian's leg deformity.

It wasn't until 1789, however, that the first clinical description of polio appeared. A British doctor named Michael Underwood wrote of a "debility of the lower extremities" in his book *Treatises on Diseases of Children*. Underwood said that the disease "usually attacks children previously reduced by fever; seldom those under one, or more than four or five years old." Underwood also made suggestions for helping the paralysis that followed the fever: "Nothing has seemed to do any good but irons [braces] to the legs, for the support of the limbs, and enabling the patient to walk."

A French illustration from 1622 depicts a probable polio survivor.

In 1813, an Italian surgeon named Giovanni Battista Monteggia published a fuller description of poliomyelitis. Under the heading "Paralysis and Atrophy," he wrote, "It [the paralysis] begins with two or three days of fever, after which one of these [lower] extremities is found quite paralyzed, immobile, flabby, hanging down and no movement is made when the sole of the foot is tickled."

In the years that followed, other doctors observed and wrote about the disease. In 1840 a German physician named Jacob von Heine made a detailed study of polio and published his findings. Heine was an orthopedist, a doctor who treats injured or diseased bones and muscles. During his career, Heine observed many cases of infantile paralysis that started with fever, vomiting, and pain. He hypothesized that the symptoms of the disease "point[ed] to an affection of the central nervous system, namely the spinal cord." He made recommendations for treatment of the paralysis, including exercise, warm baths, and the use of braces. Heine also said the malady was contagious.

Thirty years later, a French physician named Jean-Martin

Charcot analyzed microscopic samples of spinal-cord tissue taken from the corpse of a woman who had been paralyzed by an illness when she was two. Charcot, who later became famous as the founder of modern neurology, discovered that the anterior horn tissue was badly damaged. Additional autopsies on similarly paralyzed people confirmed Charcot's findings. Heine's suspicions that the disease affected the spinal cord had proven correct.

ON THE HEELS OF THE INDUSTRIAL REVOLUTION

Heine, Charcot, and other physicians studied polio during a time of great change in western Europe and North America. Some of those social changes altered the way polio spread, turning a rare disease into one that began attacking in epidemic proportions.

During the Industrial Revolution, between 1750 and 1850, many countries made the tremendous shift from agricultural to industrial economies, thanks in part to inventions that greatly changed the textile, coal, and iron industries. For example, machines were invented to spin thread and weave cloth. No longer was cloth making a home-based business run by family members. Now textiles were made in factories housing several machines run by a crew of employees.

Meanwhile, new farming technologies allowed a few people to do the work of many—leaving great numbers of rural people unemployed. Lured by the hope of factory jobs, masses of people moved from the countryside into cities with factories.

The rapid influx of people far outstripped the cities' ability to support large populations. Hastily constructed, crowded tenement houses had inadequate insulation and ventilation; sewage systems were overwhelmed; there wasn't enough clean water for drinking or washing. Disease, destitution, and death were the lot of many urban poor people. In some countries, the population in major factory towns continued to grow only because the number of rural immigrants was greater than the number of factory workers who died.

Although the living conditions throughout most industrialized cities were bad, the slums where workers lived were particularly terrible. There was no running water; lucky tenement dwellers obtained their water from a common pump in the central courtyard, while others had to fetch water in pails from rivers, lakes, or reservoirs. Sewer pipes and outhouses often emptied directly into those bodies of water. Garbage and human waste were tossed out of windows, coating the streets with a permanent, foul-smelling sludge. Smoke and soot from the nearby factories permeated the air, while factory by-products such as fabric dye contaminated the water.

Disease raged through filthy, overcrowded slums in the eighteenth and nineteenth centuries.

Diseases such as tuberculosis, typhoid, smallpox, and cholera ran rampant in the slums. Cholera, caused by bacteria that thrive in sewage-polluted water, killed thousands in Europe and North America in the first half of the nineteenth century. By comparison, the handful of crippling polio cases reported each year was hardly noteworthy.

Then, in 1854, the link between polluted water and cholera was established. Fueled by this discovery—as well as several years' worth of statistics that showed that the living conditions in slums were killing people—government officials began to focus on public health. Slowly but steadily, sewer systems were updated, water supplies were cleaned up, and sanitation improved.

Ironically, while these measures reduced the incidence of many sewage-borne illnesses, they opened the door for the polio epidemics. Before the sewage systems were improved—when everyone was constantly exposed to polluted water—most people

Playing in contaminated water spread poliovirus, a waterborne disease.

caught poliovirus as infants. In these very young children, poliovirus usually provoked only mild symptoms, if any. Those infants then had lifelong immunity, and cases of polio in older children and adults were rare. But as public water supplies were cleaned up, fewer people were exposed to polio in infancy.

The trouble was, people *were* still exposed—eventually. Now people might go years—until they were school-age children, teenagers, or adults—before encountering poliovirus. They might become infected when they interacted with someone who had the virus—an asymptomatic carrier, for example—or when they came into contact with contaminated water. So polio actually became a major public health menace *after* water supplies were cleaned up and public sanitation was improved.

In the late nineteenth and early twentieth centuries, there was a sharp rise in the number of older people crippled by polio. Today we know that the rise occurred because of the changes in social conditions. Back then, however, doctors were at a loss to explain why the disease was suddenly striking in epidemic proportions. They only knew that they couldn't cure or prevent it from crippling, even killing, their patients.

CHAPTER TWO

THE EARLY YEARS OF POLIO RESEARCH

ONE NIGHT, I HAVE BEEN TOLD, I SHOWED GREAT RELUCTANCE TO BE CAUGHT

AND PUT TO BED, AND AFTER BEING CHASED ABOUT THE ROOM,

WAS APPREHENDED AND CONSIGNED TO MY DORMITORY WITH SOME DIFFICULTY.

IT WAS THE LAST TIME I WAS TO SHOW MUCH PERSONAL AGILITY.

—*Sir Walter Scott (1771–1832), author and childhood polio survivor*

he first epidemics of poliomyelitis occurred in the second half of the nineteenth century. Compared to what was to come, these epidemics seem small, almost insignificant. But to the doctors and patients experiencing them, the outbreaks were a source of fear and confusion. They were also a source of information about a little studied and poorly understood disease.

Most towns usually recorded no more than one or two cases of polio a year. Then, in a district outside Oslo, Norway, fourteen cases were recorded in 1868. Five of the fourteen people died; the others were diagnosed with having a "light and unimportant form" of the same disease. The doctor who treated the victims,

Sir Walter Scott survived polio, but his right leg was left lame.

A. C. Bull, believed the malady to be spinal meningitis, but medical historians have since concluded that it was polio.

Bull's report also mentioned his belief that the disease was not contagious—a mistake that countless other doctors and epidemiologists (scientists who study how diseases spread) would make for the next thirty-five years. Because Bull did not recognize that the disease was contagious, he didn't realize that the "light and unimportant form" of the illness helped spread the infection as readily as the more deadly form. In fact, the fourteen patients Bull treated were probably only a small portion of those infected.

A second outbreak hit Scandinavia in 1881. Thirteen cases were reported in the small village of Umeå, Sweden. In 1887, forty-four cases were reported in the city of Stockholm. This was the greatest number ever diagnosed at one time. The outbreak was even more puzzling because many of the afflicted were school-age children, not infants.

Karl Oskar Medin, a Swedish pediatrician, investigated the Stockholm epidemic. With so many cases, he could study the disease in various stages and degrees of severity at the same time. Medin categorized the forty-four cases into different types of paralysis, depending on which part of the body was affected. In addition, he observed that patients who became paralyzed suffered two bouts of fever. The first fever only seemed to make the patient feel sick. After the second fever the patient became paralyzed. Medin came to the conclusion that during the second fever the patient's central nervous system was affected.

Medin's clinical observations, the most extensive ever made of the disease, gave him a place in the history books. Medin also taught pediatrics—including his study of polio—at the Karolinska Institute in Stockholm. One of his students, Ivar Wickman, would one day make great contributions to the medical world's understanding of polio.

The next epidemic occurred in 1894 in North America. In Rutland, Vermont, 132 residents suffered "an acute nervous disease, which was almost invariably attended with some paralysis," according to Dr. Charles Caverly, who kept meticulous records of the epidemic. A quarter of the "infantile paralysis" patients were six years old or older. Thirty of the victims became permanently paralyzed. Eighteen died, giving the epidemic a death rate of approximately 13 percent. Like the doctors before him, Caverly failed to recognize that polio was contagious. In fact, it would be more than ten years before the possibility that polio was contagious was seriously considered.

DR. IVAR WICKMAN

Although German orthopedist Jacob von Heine had first suggested that polio was contagious in 1840, few doctors followed his train of thought. Then, fifty-five years later, Karl Medin's former student Dr. Ivar Wickman resurrected Heine's suggestion.

Early in his career, Wickman witnessed two small polio epidemics: one in Stockholm in 1899, another in Göteborg in 1903. He began to ponder a few unanswered questions about the malady, which he called Heine-Medin disease, after the two researchers. What caused the illness? Was the disease contagious, passed on through direct contact? While he never discovered the answer to the first question, he became convinced that the answer to the second was yes. In 1905, a widespread epidemic struck several remote rural communities in Sweden. Wickman set out to study it.

The pioneers of polio research *(from left to right)*: Jacob von Heine, Karl Oskar Medin, Ivar Wickman, and Karl Landsteiner.

Like other doctors before him, Wickman kept close and careful records of the epidemic. But unlike these others, Wickman decided to gather information about the mild polio cases as well as the severe ones. If the disease was contagious, these mild cases were important, for they would be capable of spreading the disease.

As Wickman recorded incidences of the infection throughout Sweden, he found out that mild cases of the disease occurred much more frequently than most doctors realized. Because the symptoms of fever, headache, and nausea could easily be attributed to other illnesses, many cases of polio had gone unrecognized.

With the mild cases included, Wickman's records showed a clear pattern of dissemination—the path the disease took as it spread. Wickman recorded that outbreaks had occurred near railway stops and along main roads. This suggested that travelers spread the infection. Wickman reasoned that people infected with mild cases of the disease were much more likely to be traveling than those with severe cases. Therefore, people with mild cases could be spreading the disease.

Wickman also noted the incidence of the disease within communities. In one village, twelve out of eighteen patients were children who went to the same school. Eleven of these cases were mild. Wickman believed such data added up to one logical conclusion: polio was highly contagious, and mild cases were as capable of spreading the disease as severe cases.

Wickman's work was a giant step forward in the study of polio. Yet within three years, it would be eclipsed by a discovery that forever changed the field of poliomyelitis research.

THE BATTLE AGAINST POLIO

LANDSTEINER AND POPPER

On December 18, 1908, at a medical conference in Vienna, Austria, two scientists announced that they had identified the agent that caused polio. Karl J. Landsteiner and his assistant, Erwin Popper, said the agent was a virus.

How did Landsteiner and Popper support their discovery? Unlike bacteria, viruses are so small that they cannot be seen using even the most powerful light microscope. No one would see a virus until the electron microscope was invented in the 1930s. But scientists in the late 1800s had deduced the existence of pathogens even smaller than bacteria, called viruses. Using methods developed by the renowned bacteriologist (a scientist who studies bacteria) Dr. Robert Koch, Landsteiner and Popper proved that polio was caused by a virus.

Koch had isolated many disease-causing bacteria, including the one responsible for cholera. In 1884, he set down rules for scientists to use in figuring out what microbe caused a given disease. Known as Koch's postulates, these rules are still followed by scientists today. First, scientists had to find the microbe in every subject who had the disease. Second, they had to reproduce several generations of the microbe in a pure culture in a laboratory.

Dr. Karl Landsteiner examines microbes in his laboratory.

Third, microbes from one of these later generations had to cause the same disease when injected into experimental animals. And finally, the same microbe had to be recovered from samples taken from the experimental animals.

Landsteiner, who was to win the Nobel Prize in 1930 for his work classifying human blood types, was well schooled in Koch's postulates. He and Popper began with fluid containing spinal cord tissue from a nine-year-old boy who had died of polio. They strained the tissue through a filter small enough to trap bacteria. Then they cultured the filtered substance to see if any bacteria would grow. None did. Landsteiner and Popper now knew that the filtrate was bacteria free. Then they injected the filtrate into laboratory rabbits, guinea pigs, and mice. The scientists hoped the animals would begin to show symptoms of polio. If they did, then Landsteiner and Popper would know that something in the filtrate was causing the sickness. But the animals remained healthy.

Landsteiner and Popper persisted. They knew that rabbits, guinea pigs, and mice were very different from humans and that it was possible these animals were not susceptible to polio. The scientists couldn't perform their experiments on human subjects, of course, so they settled on a close relative: monkeys.

Obtaining monkeys for experimentation was costly and difficult, especially for two young scientists who had yet to make names for themselves. Landsteiner and Popper managed to get two rhesus monkeys who were veterans of experiments in other labs. The researchers didn't know it, but getting those monkeys was a stroke of pure luck.

Scientists divide monkeys into two families. Old World monkeys, such as the rhesus monkey, come from Asia, Africa, and Europe. New World monkeys come from Mexico, South America, and Central America and include marmosets and tamarins. Separated by oceans nearly eleven million years ago, Old World and New World monkeys developed along different evolutionary paths. There are differences in their appearances, their teeth, and their tails. And there is one other difference: Old World monkeys are susceptible to polio; New World monkeys are not. Had Landsteiner and Popper obtained New World monkeys, their

experiments would have failed. Instead, the tests were a success.

The scientists injected their monkeys with the same filtrate they had used on the other laboratory animals. Within ten days, one of the monkeys sickened and died. The other monkey succumbed in little more than two weeks, after developing complete paralysis in both legs. When Landsteiner and Popper performed autopsies on the monkeys, they found what they had hoped to find: lesions, or injuries, on the monkeys' spinal cords like those seen in human polio victims. There could be only one conclusion. Something in the filtrate from the nine-year-old boy had given the monkeys polio. Landsteiner and Popper had already ruled out bacteria, so the agent had to be a virus.

According to Koch's postulates, Landsteiner and Popper's next step should have been to transmit the disease from the dead monkeys to other test subjects. But doing so would have taken money they didn't have. Landsteiner and Popper decided their evidence was strong enough to present without more experiments.

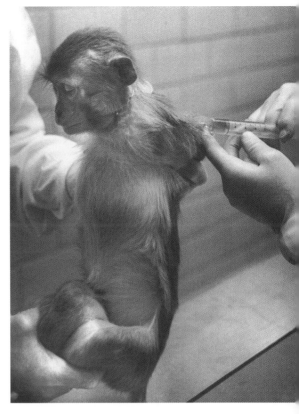

Monkeys were the subjects of many scientific experiments, including polio research.

Their choice proved wise. After hearing Landsteiner and Popper's presentation and seeing slides of the lesions at the conference in Vienna, many medical researchers returned to their labs determined to perform similar experiments. Over the next three years, the original results were repeatedly confirmed.

DR. SIMON FLEXNER

The first scientist to confirm Landsteiner's experiments was Dr. Simon Flexner of New York. A prominent physician and a well-known and respected authority in the field of bacteriology, Flexner had been appointed to a committee to study a polio epidemic that affected 750 New Yorkers in 1907.

Flexner was the director of the Rockefeller Institute for Medical Research in New York City. When the epidemic struck in 1907, he turned his attention to polio. Flexner and his colleagues were still studying the outbreak in 1908, when news of Landsteiner and Popper's discovery hit the scientific community.

Flexner realized what a breakthrough this was in the field of polio research. He quickly set about conducting his own experiments, and succeeded in giving his rhesus monkeys the disease not only with tissue solutions from human polio victims but also from other monkeys he'd infected in the laboratory.

Dr. Flexner was a highly confident and influential individual. By 1911, he was considered the world's leading authority on poliomyelitis. He was apparently sure enough of his research to run the following press release in the *The New York Times:*

Dr. Simon Flexner pushed polio into the forefront of medical research.

New York. March 9.—The Rockefeller Institute in this city believes that its search for a cure for infantile paralysis is about to be rewarded. Within six months, according to Dr. Simon Flexner, definite announcement of a specific remedy may be expected.

"We have already discovered how to prevent the disease," says Dr. Flexner in a statement published here today, "and the achievement of a cure, I may conservatively say, is not now far distant. . . . We have learned where it [the germ] resides, how the disease is spread, how the germ enters the body, the main sources of infection and the means of combating the disease."

Few people chose to contradict the findings of such a powerful figure as Simon Flexner. Unfortunately, however, one of his basic conclusions was incorrect. Flexner's experiments with the monkeys had led him to believe that the virus first attacked the respiratory system before moving on to the central nervous system. This was true in monkeys—but not in humans, in whom poliovirus first infects the digestive tract. But using humans for the early stages of experimentation was unthinkable. It would be decades before researchers realized the error.

Still, Flexner's drive to unravel the mystery of polio helped bring the disease to the forefront of medical research. Between 1909 and 1912, remarkable discoveries were made at the Rockefeller Institute and in Europe. One such discovery, made nearly simultaneously in the United States, Germany, and Austria in 1910, was that serum taken from patients recovering from polio and mixed with material containing live virus could neutralize the virus. (Serum is the thin clear liquid containing antibodies that can be separated from other parts of the blood.)

Although it would be years before a polio vaccine was developed, the experiments with serum encouraged scientists to believe that a vaccine would be possible. As the first decade of the twentieth century gave way to the second, the need for such a vaccine was becoming critical.

CHAPTER THREE

POLIO ON THE RISE

BEING CRIPPLED IS NOT LIKE MANY OTHER DISEASES, CONTAGIOUS AND

OTHERWISE, WHERE THE CURE CAN BE MADE IN A COMPARATIVELY SHORT TIME;

NOT LIKE THE MEDICAL OPERATION WHERE ONE GOES TO THE HOSPITAL

AND AT THE END OF A FEW WEEKS GOES OUT MADE OVER AGAIN AND READY

TO RESUME LIFE. PEOPLE WHO ARE CRIPPLED TAKE A LONG TIME

TO BE PUT BACK ON THEIR FEET—SOMETIMES YEARS, AS WE ALL KNOW.

—*Franklin Delano Roosevelt*

Radio Address on a Program of Assistance for the Crippled,

February 18, 1931

he scientific community had made great leaps forward in its understanding of poliomyelitis by 1910. Doctors and scientists knew that a virus caused polio, and that the disease was highly infectious. They knew that in serious cases, the virus attacked the central nervous system, leaving recognizable lesions in certain places of the spinal cord.

They also knew that outbreaks of the paralyzing disease were occurring with increasing frequency and that older people were being infected in greater numbers. In 1910, an outbreak occurred in Mason City, Iowa. In the summer of 1911, Cincinnati, Ohio, fell victim. That same summer, the biggest polio epidemic yet struck Sweden. Nearly four thousand cases were reported in this

The mother of a polio victim in 1916 gives her child a breath of fresh air.

sparsely populated country. Polio visited the United States again in 1912, striking in Buffalo, New York, as well as in the nearby town of Batavia.

All of these epidemics sent the public into a panic and medical researchers into a frenzy of investigation. While the researchers' findings helped confirm what was already known about polio, the studies were unable to determine how the virus entered the body and how it was passed from person to person.

Finding answers to these questions became imperative in 1916, when the deadliest epidemic to date hit the United States.

NEW YORK CITY EPIDEMIC, 1916

New York City is divided into five boroughs, or areas: Manhattan, Queens, the Bronx, Staten Island, and Brooklyn. It was in this last borough that the polio epidemic of 1916 began. The disease didn't stay in Brooklyn for long, however. It traveled to all five boroughs and beyond, primarily afflicting people in the Northeast, but eventually spreading throughout the United States.

The epidemic started in July and continued through November, with most cases reported during July and August. Before the epidemic ended, more than 27,000 people nationwide were diagnosed and more than 7,000 had died. Of those 27,000, more than 9,000 lived in New York City; of the 7,000 dead, 2,400

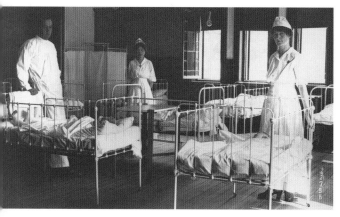

were New Yorkers also. Children under age five formed the highest percentage of the victims in the 1916 epidemic.

The epidemic sent New Yorkers into a panic. In the early days, parents desperate to keep their children safe flooded train stations and swarmed the roads in an effort to flee the disease. Some probably unknowingly carried the virus to other parts of the country.

Doctors and nurses cared for hundreds of young patients during the 1916 epidemic.

Doctors and health officials began a frantic search for the origin of the virus and the means by which it was spread. They followed a standard system of research, used many times in past decades during health crises. The first objective was to pinpoint where the disease had first taken root, then to identify a pattern in how it spread. Meanwhile, measures to contain the disease were put into place.

Crowds, hoping to escape the disease, press onto a train departing New York City.

Health officials began their search in Brooklyn, the birthplace of the epidemic. New York City, then as now, was home to many immigrants. The epidemic had started within the large Italian immigrant community in Brooklyn.

At first, native New Yorkers blamed the immigrants for the epidemic, believing they must have brought the disease from Italy. Many native New Yorkers were prejudiced against the immigrants, who were poor and lived in crowded, unsanitary conditions. In addition, some resented immigrant workers for taking scarce jobs.

It soon became clear, however, that the Italians in Brooklyn were the first victims of the epidemic, not its cause. In Italy, the government reported no recent cases of polio. Officials on

THE BATTLE AGAINST POLIO

Ellis Island, the doorway for immigrants into New York, also reported that according to its records no Italians infected with polio had entered the country.

As the disease spread to the other boroughs, city authorities hypothesized that polio thrived in filth, like cholera and other diseases. If so, eliminating filth should eliminate polio. New York City mayor John P. Mitchell ordered the streets cleaned up and garbage collected and disposed of carefully. But new polio cases continued to occur.

At about the same time as the city cleanup, the mayor turned to a centuries-old practice, quarantine, to try to stem polio's spread. Quarantine is the act of isolating individuals infected with a contagious disease to prevent them from passing on the infection. On July 14, the mayor restricted travel among the boroughs as well as to communities outside of the city. Children sixteen years old and younger were not allowed to leave New York unless they could produce a city-issued health certificate confirming that their home was free of polio. Theaters, movie houses, playgrounds, city pools, and other public places were shut down.

In addition, Mayor Mitchell gave parents of sick children two equally terrifying options. First, they could set up a completely sanitary and isolated room in their home in which to care for their young one. Most parents had no idea how to nurse a sick child infected with a potentially crippling, even deadly, disease. Fear for their children's lives, combined with a sense of their own helplessness, filled parents with despair and dread.

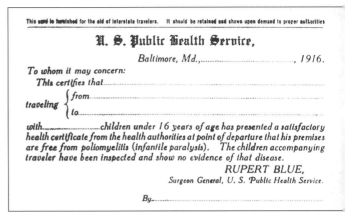

This card is furnished for the aid of interstate travelers. It should be retained and shown upon demand to proper authorities

U. S. Public Health Service,

Baltimore, Md., _____, 1916.

To whom it may concern:
  This certifies that _____

traveling { from _____
          { to _____

with _____ children under 16 years of age has presented a satisfactory health certificate from the health authorities at point of departure that his premises are free from poliomyelitis (infantile paralysis). The children accompanying traveler have been inspected and show no evidence of that disease.
          RUPERT BLUE,
  Surgeon General, U. S. Public Health Service.

  By _____

Adults with young travelers had to show a certificate declaring their home and children to be free of polio.

A reluctant mother hands her polio-stricken child to ambulance drivers for the trip to the hospital.

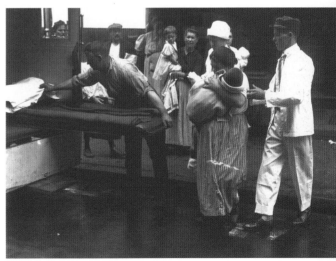

Yet to many, the mayor's second option seemed worse. Mitchell decreed that anyone unable to set up an isolation room had to bring their sick child to the hospital. In the early twentieth century, hospitals were not the sterile, high-tech establishments of today. People entered hospitals only as a last resort, because they could not afford to be treated by a doctor at home—or because they were dying.

During the 1916 epidemic, hospital wards were full of destitute, crippled, and dying polio patients. For many people, handing their young children over to strangers to be placed in a room with such people was worse than keeping the infected child at home. In fact, many who couldn't set up the required isolation rooms, usually poorer families and immigrants, tried to hide their children from authorities. When they were found out, the children—some as young as one and two years old, most suffering terrible pain and terrified at being separated from their parents—were taken by force to the hospitals.

Animals were exterminated in a vain attempt to control polio's spread.

People might have been more cooperative if the quarantine had any effect. But it appeared that polio was immune to quarantine.

At one point, people thought perhaps animals carried polio, as they did rabies (a viral disease that causes headaches, vomiting, and even death if untreated). Desperate for action, the panicked citizenry slaughtered thousands of rats, mice, stray dogs and cats, and even pets. A newspaper reported that 350 cats were killed in one week; by the end of July, the number of dead felines had reached 72,000. Still the epidemic marched on.

If animals weren't passing the disease, perhaps insects were. Yellow fever, a deadly illness that had swept the southern United States in the late 1800s, had been spread by mosquitoes that carried the disease-causing germ. People noted that polio epidemics came in summer, when the insect populations were active. But measures taken to kill mosquitoes proved worthless.

While medical authorities struggled to provide an answer to the origin of the epidemic, members of the public offered their own opinions. "The poisonous gases used in the war in Europe and the germs from the dead bodies there are breathed by the sharks," one New York woman affirmed. "The sharks carry these germs to America and breathe them into the air. The air is inhaled by people who are affected by the germs and gases. Children are the chief victims of this disease because they are the weakest."

Some people claimed tarantulas had injected the virus into bananas that were shipped to New York. Other suspect foods included ice cream, soda, and candy. A number of people were sure that radio waves had bombarded children and caused their paralysis.

If these suggestions seem bizarre now, they were no worse than some experts' theories. Health authorities, casting about for patterns in the way the disease spread, noticed early on that African-American children seemed to be immune. An extension of this theory claimed that blond children were more susceptible than dark-haired children. One doctor even believed that children's stature, the shape of their faces, and the position of their teeth determined how susceptible they were! But as the disease continued to run rampant, and hospital wards filled with children of all colors, shapes, and sizes, it became clear that polio made no such distinctions.

When the epidemic finally abated in November of 1916, the authorities had ruled out several means of transmission—animals and insects didn't spread the disease, and filth didn't appear to

I am the Baby-Killer!
I come from garbage-cans uncovered,
From gutter pools and filth of streets,
From stables and backyards neglected,
Slovenly homes—all manner of unclean places.
I love to crawl on babies' bottles and baby lips;
I love to wipe my poison feet on open food
In stores and markets patronized by fools.

Could it be that flies and filth spread the disease? A 1916 newspaper cartoon makes a creepy statement about cleanliness.

breed it—and had gained further evidence that polio was highly contagious. But they still didn't know enough to stop future outbreaks.

FRANKLIN DELANO ROOSEVELT

After 1916, polio didn't strike in epidemic proportions for nearly fifteen years. Outbreaks still occurred, but they didn't affect the huge numbers of people the 1916 epidemic had. While children continued to be the most common targets, polio also struck adults in the prime of their lives.

Franklin Delano Roosevelt, president of the United States from 1933 to 1945 (during the Great Depression and World War II) and engineer of landmark social programs, was an adult victim of paralysis. He was instrumental in raising the profile of polio and in providing help for its victims.

In the summer of 1921, Roosevelt was on vacation with his wife, Eleanor, and their five children on Campobello Island, off the coast of New Brunswick, Canada. The future president was thirty-nine years old and had recently lost a bid for the vice presidency. The campaign had been exhausting; he hoped the vacation would rejuvenate him.

Instead, Roosevelt became sick. "First symptoms of the illness appeared in August 1921," he wrote three years later, "when I was thoroughly tired from overwork. I first had a chill in the evening which lasted practically all night. The following morning the muscles of the right knee appeared weak and by afternoon I was unable to support my weight on my right leg. That evening the left knee began to weaken also and by the following morning I was unable to stand up. . . . By the end of the third day practically all muscles from the chest down were involved."

At first, a local doctor told Roosevelt that his symptoms were caused by a blood clot lodged in his spine. The doctor assured him that he would make a full and speedy recovery when the clot shifted. He instructed Eleanor to give her husband deep massages to help dislodge the clot.

As the days passed, the Roosevelts realized with growing dread that the malady had been misdiagnosed. The massages were not only ineffective, they were agonizing. The paralysis soon spread to his arms, hands, and upper trunk. The Roosevelts had lived through the New York City epidemic of 1916. They asked polio specialist Dr. Robert W. Lovett of Boston to come to Campobello Island. Lovett immediately confirmed their fears: FDR had polio; his paralysis could be permanent.

In the months that followed, the Roosevelt family adjusted to coping with FDR's condition. Eleanor met the emotionally and physically challenging task of caring for an adult invalid. Fearing that FDR could pass the illness on, she instructed her children to stay clear of their father. The closest they were allowed to come was the threshold of his bedroom door.

Despite his agony, Roosevelt always tried to appear light-hearted. "Father was unbelievably concerned about how we would take it," wrote FDR's son James. "He grinned at us, and he did his best to call out, or gasp out, some cheery response to our tremulous, just-this-side-of-tears greeting."

FDR showed the world this same cheerful face once his illness was made public. News of it broke when he was moved from Campobello Island to his home in Hyde Park, New York. However, he made sure that very few knew the extent of his paralysis. Despite the prospect of permanent immobility, Roosevelt hadn't given up his dream of becoming a leader in national politics.

During the winter of 1921–1922, he regained use of his upper body and arms, but his legs remained paralyzed. Roosevelt, a man of great determination, set a goal to walk again. He kept up a

FDR'S DIAGNOSIS: TRUE OR FALSE?

In the November 2003 issue of the *Journal of Medical Biography,* a small group of doctors and medical historians from Texas published an article that claimed history was wrong. Franklin Delano Roosevelt did not have polio, they said. He had a rare syndrome now known as Guillain-Barré.

Dr. Armond Goldman, a professor emeritus of the University of Texas Medical Branch, sparked the study into FDR's medical history. He believed it was unlikely that a man as old as FDR—thirty-nine at the time of his illness—would contract a disease that typically struck young children. But if FDR didn't have polio, what caused his paralysis?

Guillain-Barré syndrome shares many of polio's symptoms, including muscle weakness and paralysis that starts with the lower body and moves upward. Unlike polio, however, Guillain-Barré does not appear to be the result of a virus or any other disease-causing agent. This is why it is called a syndrome rather than a disease.

The syndrome can afflict anyone at any age. It occurs when the body's own immune system attacks the central nervous system. Such an attack comes after the immune system has fought off an infection of the digestive or respiratory sys-

FDR, shown wearing his leg braces while fishing.

tem. At this point, doctors still haven't figured out why the immune system goes haywire, although some speculate that the infection may change the very nature of the cells that fight off disease. Fortunately, the syndrome is very rare—only one in one hundred thousand will be afflicted—and chances for recovery are very good.

After examining FDR's medical records and his own personal account of his disease and paralysis, Dr. Goldman and his team came to believe the president was one of the unlucky ones who didn't make a full recovery. So far, their conclusions have met with resistance from medical historians and FDR biographers alike. And Goldman himself admits his team's results are inconclusive. "I can't tell you he didn't have paralytic polio. That would be foolhardy of me," he says. "But I don't think he did."

In the end, exactly what caused Roosevelt's paralysis doesn't change history. He believed he had polio and, in the years following his affliction, he became one of the nation's most outspoken leaders in the fight against the disease. It's possible that without his constant support, that fight would have gone on much longer.

steady correspondence with polio experts and fellow victims. He researched treatment for polio sufferers and finally arrived at a routine. Each day he would exercise his upper body by dragging himself back and forth across the floor, sometimes sitting, sometimes on his stomach. He used his arms to push himself backward up four flights of stairs, one step at a time. Holding himself up with his arms between parallel bars, he dragged himself—step by step, one leg then the other—from one end of the bars to the other. With leg braces and crutches, he would "walk" with lurching steps down his driveway, trying to cover its two-hundred-yard length.

Roosevelt worked hard to develop his upper-body muscles.

In October of 1924, Roosevelt's rehabilitation took a new turn. During his research into cures for polio, he learned that many health care experts believed immersion in pools fed by natural hot springs could help paralysis and other muscle conditions. With this in mind, FDR journeyed to Warm Springs, Georgia. Warm Springs got its name from the warm, mineralized water that flowed down from nearby Pine Mountain. His first day there, Roosevelt worked out in the water for more than two hours. That was far longer than he had been able to exercise in Hyde Park, for the water gave him buoyancy, making exercise easier, and the warm temperature was soothing to the muscles. In the months that followed, he continued with daily hydrotherapy and became increasingly hopeful. "The legs are really improving a great deal," he wrote to Eleanor at one point. "The walking and general exercise in the water is fine and I have worked out some special exercises also. This is really a discovery of a place and there is no doubt that I've got to do it some more."

Roosevelt was so taken with Warm Springs that he bought the

property in the spring of 1926 and turned it into a nonprofit rehabilitation center called the Georgia Warm Springs Foundation. The foundation, which relied on grants and fellowships, charged its patients only minimal fees. The chief purpose of Warm Springs was to help polio victims, and numerous clients left the facility feeling better than when they had entered.

Despite his efforts, Roosevelt never regained use of his legs. For the rest of his life, he was confined to a wheelchair. His determination to continue his political career never wavered, however. Seven years after his initial infection, Roosevelt reentered politics.

FDR was sure that if the public learned of his paralysis or saw him in a wheelchair, they would think he was incapable of providing strong leadership. So he did everything in his power to conceal the extent of his affliction—not an easy task, considering how many times he appeared in public during and after a successful campaign for the governorship of New York and, later, for the presidency.

After he was elected president, he continued to conceal his paralysis. Whenever he made a speech, he wore braces under his pants to hold himself upright and leaned on the podium or held someone's arm for support. He used a special wheelchair that closely resembled a regular kitchen chair and made sure he was not photographed in it. Today, out of more than 35,000 photographs, only two show him in his wheelchair.

Roosevelt's deception, while the subject of some controversy now, in light of the country's cry for truthful politicians, didn't affect how he ran the nation. It also didn't mean he had turned his back on polio. Quite the contrary.

In January 1938, Roosevelt established the National Foundation for Infantile Paralysis (NFIP), an association of scientists and volunteers whose purpose was to help victims of polio and to fund polio research. The name was later changed to the March of Dimes, after the foundation ran a nationwide fund-raiser that called upon the public to send donations, even amounts as small as dimes, to President Roosevelt. The money received from this fund-raiser, the first of its kind, went toward training professionals in the care and treatment of polio patients. It also paid for orthopedic equipment, therapy, and medical services for hundreds of polio sufferers. This type of fund-raising was to make life easier for countless polio victims and their families in the decades to come.

Meanwhile, a new research breakthrough was about to make it easier for scientists to continue their battle against polio.

A BRIGHT SPOT

About the same time the NFIP was established, researchers at Yale University finally discovered that poliovirus multiplied in the digestive tract, not the respiratory system. Since Dr. Simon Flexner had pronounced that polio was a respiratory ailment in 1911, no one had detected the flaw in his findings. Now, the Yale researchers reported they had found large amounts of poliovirus in the feces of polio patients. They suggested that the virus reproduced in the intestines, and was spread by contact with infected feces.

This radical suggestion, contradicting nearly thirty years of conventional wisdom, was not greeted with enthusiasm. At a meeting of the American Epidemiological Society in April 1938, a member of the audience rose and said, "For some years now we have been following the good work that the Yale unit has been doing, but now, although I am loath to say it, they have apparently gone off the deep end." It would take a year and a half and many more scientific studies of stool samples, before the truth was widely accepted.

CHAPTER FOUR

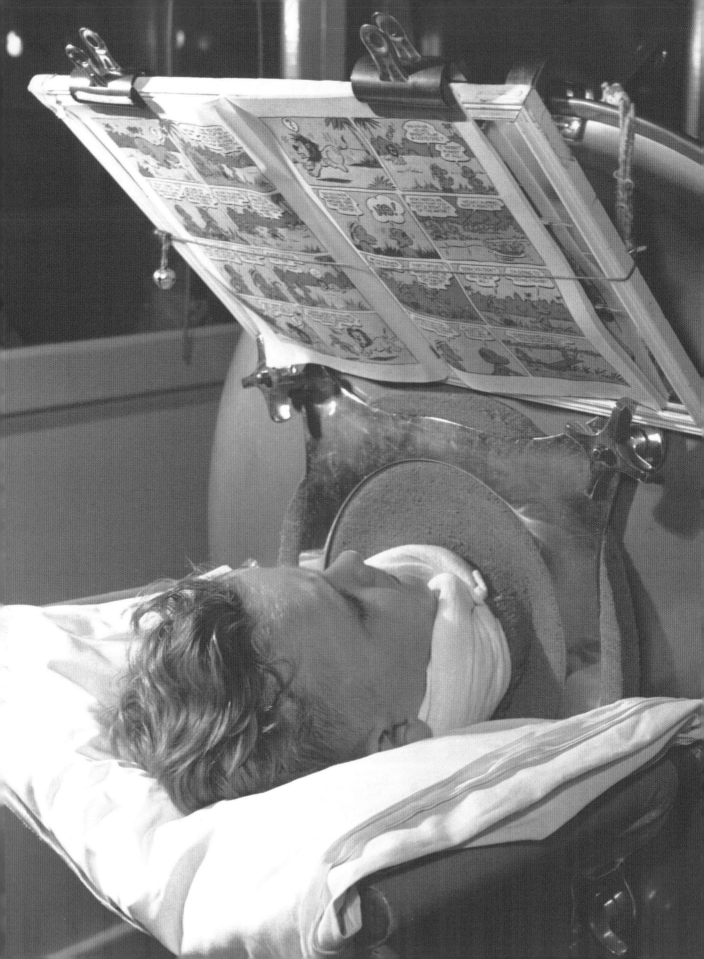

COPING
WITH THE
INCURABLE

AS I STOOD BY THE BEDSIDE OF A LOVELY CHILD NOT YET IN HER TEENS,
AND WATCHED THREE PEOPLE ATTEMPTING TO TURN HER OVER IN ONE PIECE
WHILE A LOOK OF PAIN AND FEAR CONTORTED HER FACE, I WONDERED
HOW LONG THIS TRAGEDY TO HUMANITY WOULD CONTINUE.
—*Sister Elizabeth Kenny, polio treatment pioneer, 1940*

or many decades, as polio epidemics swept over the industrialized world, thousands of children survived and grew up with polio. While a handful of doctors were doing research into the causes and trying to find ways to control polio, most physicians were simply doing their best to treat its effects and help patients cope with the illness and disability.

In the early years, a common treatment was to immobilize affected muscles with splints and plaster casts, to protect them from further injury and to help support the person after recovery from the illness. However, immobilization was clearly useless when the muscles affected were the ones that controlled breathing. In the earliest epidemics, patients who suffered from this

Opposite:

A young polio victim reads a comic book while in an iron lung.

kind of polio usually died. They could not draw breath because their lungs were not able to expand. Then, in 1927, a resourceful engineer invented a new tool that was to help doctors save thousands of lives.

THE IRON LUNG

Philip Drinker, an engineer, and his colleagues at the Harvard School of Public Health invented a respirator that enabled paralytic polio patients to breathe. The device was called the Drinker respirator when introduced in 1927; today, most people know it as the iron lung.

The iron lung consisted of a cylindrical metal tank. The polio patient lay on a bed and the tank was fitted over his or her body, leaving the head sticking out. The tank was equipped with holes, like portholes in a boat, so that therapists and caregivers could reach their patients without having to remove the apparatus.

The iron lung was connected to a pump that created a partial vacuum within the cylinder. This vacuum caused the patient's lungs to expand and fill with air—an inhalation. Then the pump released the vacuum, and the lungs relaxed and emptied—an exhalation.

Drinker's device was first tested on animals, then on premature babies who needed help breathing because their lungs were not yet fully developed. Then the respirator was adapted for young polio patients and, finally, adult polio victims. There were some setbacks early on, when the iron lung seemed to fail more often than it helped. The apparatus was cumbersome and very expensive, and some people wondered aloud if living in the artificial environment created by the iron lung was really all that much better than taking one's chances without it.

Still, as improvements were made to Drinker's design, the

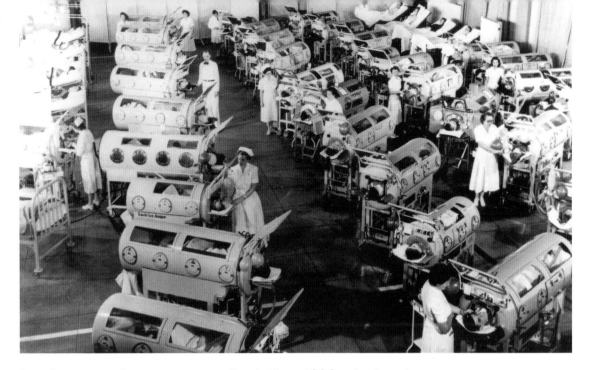

iron lung came into greater use. By the late 1930s, the iron lung was acknowledged as a lifesaver. As the incidence of polio increased, demand for iron lungs grew so great that manufacturers couldn't keep up.

At about this time, the National Foundation for Infantile Paralysis joined with one of Drinker's colleagues, Dr. James L. Wilson of the University of Michigan. Together they conceived of the concept of the "respirator center." Respirator centers were equipped with several iron lungs. Patients were brought to these centers for immediate and long-term care. In many cases, patients emerged from the iron lung after a few days or weeks. But sometimes, they lived out their lives in one. Nurses and doctors received training at the facilities to deal with these types of cases. Such centers began to appear in cities around the country, and then the world.

Once patients lived through the agonizing initial stages of polio, there were often lengthy follow-up treatments, including corrective surgeries and numerous fittings for braces and crutches. There were also many theories about how best to combat the paralysis. When FDR was researching treatments, he was advised to try

Hospitals had to create respirator centers to house victims of paralytic polio.

everything from daily massages and soaks in saltwater baths to horseback riding to exposure to ultraviolet light. Then, in the 1930s, a new figure entered the field of polio treatment—and radically changed it, for good.

SISTER KENNY, CRUSADER AGAINST POLIO

Sister Elizabeth Kenny was born and raised in Australia. When she was a teenager, Kenny fell from her horse and broke her wrist. Her doctor, Aeneas McDonnell, set the break, then showed Kenny textbooks on how muscles worked. This chance encounter launched Kenny's lifelong fascination with the workings of the human body.

When she was old enough, Kenny left her home in Queensland to receive informal training as a nurse. In 1911, she moved to a remote area of inland Australia, known as "the bush," to provide medical treatment to the indigenous people there. When World War I started, in 1914, she left the bush to join the army as a nurse. There she acquired the designation *Sister,* the Australian title for army nurses; it stayed with her for life.

Sister Kenny had seen many cases of polio early in her career. She had also seen how doctors treated it by immobilizing affected limbs in casts and splints. In Australia as in the United States, doctors believed immobilization prevented further damage.

Sister Kenny questioned this practice, since when the casts were taken off, the patients' limbs were so weakened and stiff that they were nearly impossible to move. Sister Kenny believed that the pain polio patients suffered was caused by muscle spasms, or involuntary contractions of the muscles. Immobilizing muscles that were spasming, she believed, only ensured their inability to recover. And, since healthy muscles were usually immobilized along with the spasming ones, they would be nearly as useless with this treatment.

To her mind, a better treatment was to gently exercise, stretch, and massage the affected muscles. She also tried applying hot, wet, lightweight packs to the limbs to soothe and relax the muscles and promote blood flow. She used these methods with great success. "I want them rags that wells my legs!" a young female patient once begged Sister Kenny.

Despite her many success stories, most medical professionals scoffed at Sister Kenny's treatments. Some voiced their opposition in strident tones. Sister Kenny later wrote of "the extraordinary attitude of the medical world in its readiness to condemn anything that smacked of reform or that ran contrary to approved methods of practice." She further wondered "how many promising discoveries have been consigned to oblivion without being given an opportunity to prove their worth."

Thanks to Sister Kenny's method, this polio sufferer regained the use of her legs.

Undaunted, Sister Kenny in 1933 opened her own polio treatment clinic in Townsville, New South Wales. For the next five years, she worked hard to convince doctors in Australia that her methods were sound. She also developed the Kenny Method, a routine of stretches, exercises, massage, and the application of hot, wet compresses. Gradually, some physicians began to take her side, but most still rejected her. In 1938, 130 doctors condemned her practices in an official report.

Then, in the first week of September 1939, progress came to a standstill, though not because of anything Kenny or her opposition had done. On September 1, World War II began when Germany invaded Poland. Australia entered the war two days later.

Sister Kenny soon realized that if she was to continue her crusade, she needed to be where the medical community was not embroiled in World War II. The United States was the obvious choice, for two reasons. First, it had not yet entered the war, although the government and President Roosevelt were keeping close watch on the events in Europe. Second, the United States continued to suffer through frequent outbreaks of polio.

On April 14, 1940, Sister Kenny, now sixty years old, arrived in San Francisco. She was armed with letters of introduction from the Australian health ministry. The letters helped her establish contact with hospitals and eventually led her to Minneapolis, Minnesota, and the University of Minnesota. There she met with doctors from several area hospitals. The doctors had heard of her work and were interested.

They were even more interested once they had seen a demonstration. Kenny removed casts and splints from several patients. At first, the patients were unable to bend their limbs, but after several sessions of therapy, they began to improve. Their muscles became more flexible. Some even regained full use of "paralyzed" limbs.

Soon, word of Kenny's success spread like wildfire throughout the medical world. So convincing were her results that in December 1941, the NFIP officially endorsed her techniques. One year later, on December 17, 1942, she opened the Sister Elizabeth Kenny Institute in Minneapolis to train people in the Kenny Method.

Any lingering doubts of the country's acceptance of the Kenny Method were dispelled in 1943. On June 8, Sister Kenny was invited to meet another leader in the fight against polio. "I was informed that the President of the United States of America wished to have me lunch with him at the White House," Kenny wrote in her autobiography. "It must be confessed that I was inordinately excited at the prospect."

Within a few short years, American doctors had almost completely abandoned the practice of immobilization in favor of Kenny's techniques. Doctors in the rest of the world followed suit. She received numerous medals and commendations, as well as countless letters of thanks from patients and their parents, including photographs of "Kenny Method children" who were now walking, running, and dancing. By 1952, the year of her death, Kenny had the satisfaction of knowing that she had revolutionized treatment for polio patients.

Sister Kenny's revolutionary treatments saved many polio victims from being permanently paralyzed.

ORDINARY PEOPLE, EXTRAORDINARY LIVES

"Torture time." That's what children's book author Peg Schulze Kehret called the Kenny Method therapy she went through after being paralyzed with polio at age twelve. "I was pushed up until I sat upright in bed, with my legs out in front of me," she wrote in her book *Small Steps*. A nurse would then press her head down toward her knees. "The pain began at the back of my neck and ran all the way down my spine and along the backs of both legs. . . . I thought I could not bear it." She would endure such painful sessions throughout the next year. Luckily, she didn't suffer in vain. By the year's end, she was able to walk again.

Dick Owen's experience with polio treatment was very different from Peg Kehret's. Stricken with the disease in 1940, when the Kenny Method had yet to become the norm, Dick was immobilized for months. "I was kept on a frame made of canvas strapped across a metal bar," Owen recalled. "I was then put in Toronto splints, which were leather-covered splints that kept the knees bent, the feet pulled out a little bit, and the legs spread

WILMA RUDOLPH: TRIUMPH OVER POLIO

Wilma Glodean Rudolph was born on June 23, 1940, in Clarksville, Tennessee. She was a small, sickly baby who was not expected to live. But from the start, Wilma was a determined girl. She not only lived, she overcame great odds to become one of the world's outstanding female athletes.

When Wilma was four, she came down with polio and lost the use of her left leg. Wilma's doctor informed Blanche Rudolph, Wilma's mother, that Wilma would never walk again.

Blanche refused to accept this. She began taking Wilma for Kenny Method therapy sessions at Meharry Hospital, a facility that, unlike many hospitals in the 1940s, treated African Americans. Meharry was fifty miles away from Clarksville, yet Blanche still managed to get Wilma there twice a week. The exercises were painful, but Wilma rarely complained.

Polio survivor Wilma Rudolph wins the gold medal in 1960.

The determination and hard work of mother and daughter paid off. After two years, Wilma could walk with the help of a leg brace, corrective shoes, and crutches. She continued her exercises at home and, by the time she was twelve, she was able to walk on her own.

Many people would have been content with that achievement. But not Wilma. Now that she had mastered walking, she wanted to run and jump! So she tried out for her junior high school basketball team—and made it. She spent most of that first season on the bench, but still, she got to practice. And with every practice she grew stronger and faster.

Wilma eventually became a star player. Her abilities caught the eye of Ed Temple, the track coach of Tennessee State University. He told Wilma she could be a great runner and invited her to train with the university's team during summer sports camp. Wilma accepted.

Almost overnight, the girl who was never supposed to walk became one of the fastest female runners in the world. She not only shone during the summer sports camp, but earned a spot on the U.S. Olympic team! At the age of sixteen, Wilma traveled with the team to Melbourne, Australia, for the 1956 Olympic Games. When the Games were over, Wilma returned home—with a bronze medal for placing third in the 400-meter relay.

Four years later, Wilma again took part in the Olympics. This time, she won three golds—the first American woman to ever win so many first-place medals in one Olympic Games.

apart. . . . I spent a total of nine months in that situation." Interestingly, Owen would one day become the medical director of the Kenny Institute.

Many polio victims underwent surgeries and treatments aimed at correcting deformities and disabilities. "I had body wedging during four separate summers," wrote James Gary Brown on his Web site devoted to memories of growing up with polio. He experienced a combination of Kenny Method and other therapies.

The body wedging process involved wrapping the body from knee to armpit in a cast, then inserting a block of wood into the cast to force the spine into a straight line. "Each week for six weeks my back would be x-rayed to see the spinal curve. Twice each week the cast would be cut and a larger block of wood inserted," Brown recalled. "Eight weeks in a body cast for a kid who is really not ill is an experience."

Unfortunately, such experiences were common throughout the 1940s and early 1950s, for although doctors knew what caused polio and had learned how to treat patients for maximum results, they still couldn't stop the disease from striking in the first place.

CHAPTER FIVE

VACCINE TRIALS —AND ERRORS

THE FIGHT AGAINST INFANTILE PARALYSIS IS A FIGHT TO THE FINISH,

AND THE TERMS ARE UNCONDITIONAL SURRENDER.

—*President Franklin D. Roosevelt, December 1, 1944*

hroughout the 1930s and 1940s, while Sister Kenny, President Roosevelt, and the National Foundation for Infantile Paralysis were trying to help people with polio, researchers were working feverishly to understand the disease and to develop a vaccine to prevent it from infecting people in the first place.

The need for such a vaccine was obvious. Ever since the 1916 New York epidemic, outbreaks of polio had struck cities across the United States as well as in other countries nearly every summer.

Vaccination was not a new concept; the first vaccine had been successfully created in the late 1700s, when Dr. Edward Jenner inoculated humans with cowpox to create immunity to smallpox, a viral cousin to cowpox. By the 1930s, vaccines had come a long way, but they were far from an exact science. Vaccines fell into two camps: those that used a "killed" strain of the virus, in which the virus still existed but had been deactivated, and those that used a live, but weakened, strain. Both types provided immunity by causing the body to create antibodies. In 1935, one of each kind of vaccine for polio underwent the first human trials. Unfortunately, the results were disastrous.

BRODIE AND KOLMER

In the 1930s two doctors were racing each other to be the first to put his polio vaccine through human testing. Dr. Maurice Brodie had been working on a vaccine since his graduation from medical school in Montreal. He moved to New York in 1931 and by 1935, he had developed what he believed was a viable vaccine made from a killed strain of the poliovirus. In early trials, he successfully created immunity to polio in twenty laboratory monkeys.

Unfortunately, the trials were not as successful when performed on human subjects. During the summer of 1935, Brodie's vaccine was given to thousands of children. Despite his claim that "no harmful effects have developed after more than 3,000 inoculations," something went wrong that caused further trials to be abandoned. What exactly that "something" was remains a mystery to polio historians—but the fact that the Brodie vaccine was never used again points to something tragic.

At the same time Brodie was developing his killed vaccine, Dr. John A. Kolmer of Philadelphia was working on a vaccine using live, weakened poliovirus. After testing his vaccine on monkeys, then on himself, his two children, and an additional twenty-two other children, Kolmer believed he was ready to test a larger human population. Perhaps it was coincidence—or perhaps it was his desire to beat Brodie in the race for a vaccine—but Kolmer's trials also took place during the summer of 1935. Kolmer sent out twelve thousand samples of his vaccine to doctors around the nation. Then he waited. The results were swift in coming, but they were hardly to Kolmer's liking. A large number of children who were administered his vaccine became ill and many died.

Both Brodie and Kolmer were condemned for having hurried their experiments through to the human trial stage. During a November 1935 meeting of the Southern Branch of the American Public Health Association, Brodie is reported to have stood up and said, "It looks as though . . . my vaccine is no good, and . . . Dr. Kolmer's is dangerous." Kolmer expressed his regrets by saying, "Gentlemen, this is one time I wish the floor would open up and swallow me."

Brodie and Kolmer had no way of knowing that their vaccines were doomed to failure from the outset. The reason was simple: neither man knew that there were three types of poliovirus and that in order for a vaccine to be effective, it had to contain all three types. In addition, procedures used to kill and weaken poliovirus were not exact. It's probable that the poliovirus in the vaccines was stronger than either man thought. Still, had they decided to perform more extensive lab tests instead of rushing to human trials, tragedy might have been avoided.

After these two ill-fated trials, the public rebelled against using humans for experimentation. Scientists continued research on the vaccine, however. One of their goals was to figure out how to mass-produce a polio vaccine. In order to make large quantities, the researchers first had to overcome a problem they had: their inability to grow the poliovirus outside a living body. In early experiments, polio vaccines were made by harvesting poliovirus from the tissues of infected monkeys. But this was not a practical way to produce large quantities of vaccine because monkeys were expensive and required a great deal of care and space.

The problem of growing viruses was compounded by the fact that poliovirus grew in nerve tissue. When viruses from nerve tissue were used for vaccines, severe allergic reactions in children often occurred. The reactions sometimes caused brain damage. (It has been speculated that this is what went wrong with Brodie's vaccine.) So until researchers could grow poliovirus outside the body, using virus taken from tissue other than nerve tissue, mass vaccination seemed impossible.

Then, in 1948, these obstacles were overcome. John Enders, Thomas Weller, and Frederick Robbins, researchers from Harvard University, succeeded in culturing poliovirus in the laboratory. Their original virus samples were taken from monkey kidney tissue, not from nerve tissue. The team then performed experiments with the virus they had cultured—without ever introducing it into the body of an animal. When they did finally inject their culture into laboratory subjects, it was to see if the virus had multiplied and survived the experiments. It had.

Dr. John Enders and his team were the first to grow poliovirus outside a living body.

Enders, Weller, and Robbins published their findings in the journal *Science* in January 1949. Thanks to their efforts, for which they were awarded the Nobel Prize in 1954, mass production of a vaccine was possible. Now the only question remaining was, what should the vaccine consist of?

VACCINE TRIALS—AND ERRORS

THE TYPING PROGRAM

In 1948, Harry Weaver, Research Director of the NFIP, approached Basil O'Connor, the foundation's head, about funding a study of the poliovirus. Weaver and O'Connor both knew that such a study was necessary for the development of an effective vaccine. Researchers had long suspected that there were different types of poliovirus. They believed all types caused infection, but were different enough from one another that immunity to one did not guarantee immunity to the others. Therefore, in order for a vaccine to be effective, it had to contain all types of poliovirus known to infect humans.

In 1948, O'Connor authorized Weaver to organize four teams of researchers to identify and classify the different poliovirus types. This study became known as the Typing Program. One of the team leaders of the Typing Program was Dr. Jonas Salk.

Salk was an associate professor of bacteriology at the University of Pittsburgh. He had spent many years working with viruses, especially the influenza virus. He also had a great deal of experience with the development of vaccines. When the NFIP offered him and the University of Pittsburgh a grant of $200,000 to take part in the polio Typing Program, Salk signed on.

The work was tedious, but Salk understood its importance. Salk and his colleagues experimented with countless samples and analyzed reams of data. In 1951, they published their findings. They had positively identified three distinct types of poliovirus. With this indisputable information in hand, the way was clear for the development of a polio vaccine. Sadly, it would not be created in time to prevent one of the worst polio epidemics to hit the United States.

THE 1952 EPIDEMIC

In the years since the 1916 New York epidemic, many parents had viewed summertime with dread. Summer was the time of year during which most polio outbreaks occurred. Outbreaks of epidemic proportions had struck in 1936, 1937, 1941, 1944, 1946, 1949, and, most recently, in 1951. Reminders of these past polio outbreaks were everywhere. Children stricken with the disease learned to walk with braces or crutches or to maneuver wheelchairs. Posters made by the March of Dimes showed the hopeful faces of crippled children who might be helped if enough people donated to the cause. Photographs of infants encased in iron lungs were published in magazines and newspapers. As the weather warmed in 1952, people wondered if their communities would be spared the excruciating pain and suffering of polio.

Parents took measures to keep their children safe. If public pools were open, some parents forbade their children to visit them. Playgrounds were off-limits, too, as were many social gatherings

Children in the early 1950s hula-hoop to help raise money to fight polio.

such as birthday parties. Children who looked forward to going to summer camp found themselves at home instead.

City officials took their own measures. Homes of polio patients had "Polio—Keep Out!" and "Quarantine!" signs posted on them. Theaters, public pools, even churches and schools were closed at the first sign of polio in a community. Hospitals isolated polio patients from other wards, sometimes enclosing them in glass cubicles to keep the infection from spreading.

But in the summer of 1952, it seemed to many that nothing could prevent polio from striking. "There were sixteen or seventeen new admissions every day," recalled one nurse who worked the polio ward in a Pittsburgh hospital. "It was an atmosphere of grief, terror, and helpless rage. It was horrible."

The 1952 epidemic goes down in history as the largest one; all told, 57,879 people in the United States contracted polio that terrifying summer. More than 3,000 of them died, and hundreds more were left crippled or encased in iron lungs. Many victims of the 1952 epidemic are still alive today. Their memories of the days their lives changed forever are vivid.

"I can remember being on a gurney and my parents saying goodbye to me," recalled Arvid Schwartz, who was twelve when he became infected. He was "wheeled to a room amidst a lot of clatter of iron lungs, down to a room that was just wall-to-wall beds with people who had just been diagnosed. . . . I cried a lot because I had no idea what was going to happen to me. . . . I remember my mother and father standing above me and taking my hand and saying goodbye." Schwartz has used leg braces and crutches ever since.

Carol Boyer was only three when she contracted polio in 1952. "I do remember seeing a few people in iron lungs—men and women, and that was very very scary to me, to see people that

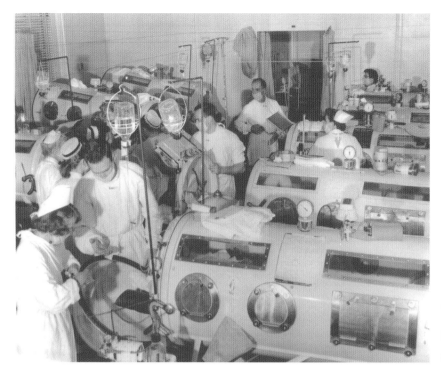

Iron lungs saved
many lives but were
terrifying machines.

had to be flat on their backs, only their heads stuck out of this
big, white, cylindrical machine. I thought they didn't have bodies."
Boyer had nightmares about those machines throughout her childhood. And although she made enough of a recovery to be able
to walk without crutches after the age of thirteen, her classmates
cruelly mocked her by mimicking her limping walk.

Arvid, Carol, and the thousands of others afflicted with polio
that year had no way of knowing that even as the epidemic raged
across the country, scientists were inching closer to a vaccine.

TIME

THE WEEKLY NEWSMAGAZINE

POLIO FIGHTER SALK

Is this the year?

ARTZYBASHEFF

CHAPTER SIX

SALK AND SABIN

WHEN YOU GIVE SOME OF THE POLIO VACCINE FOR THE FIRST TIME,
YOU JUST . . . YOU'RE ON PINS AND NEEDLES WAITING FOR THE RESULTS.

—*Dr. Jonas Salk, creator of the Salk polio vaccine, 1952*

uring his association with the Typing Program, Dr. Jonas Salk had also spent countless hours in his laboratory working to create a polio vaccine. He favored using killed poliovirus, believing it was less risky than live, weakened strains.

To create his killed virus, Salk first learned the techniques of growing live viruses, which were developed by Enders, Weller, and Robbins in 1949. Once he had enough viruses, he killed them by mixing them with formalin, a diluted form of the chemical solution formaldehyde. Formalin deactivated the virus without completely destroying it—in other words, he was left with the viral equivalent of a corpse.

Opposite:

Dr. Jonas Salk, developer of the first effective polio vaccine.

In the spring of 1952, after many months of experiments with monkeys, Salk was prepared to begin human experiments with his killed poliovirus vaccine. The subjects came from the D. T. Watson Home for Crippled Children, located just outside of Pittsburgh.

The experiment would be conducted in secrecy; only the subjects, all of whom had suffered through polio infections, and the workers at the home would know of it. Salk explained his intention to "take blood from polio patients, find out the type of antibodies they had, and then inoculate them with vaccines of the same types to see if the vaccines would raise their antibody levels." Salk added his reassurance that "since the subjects already had antibody and were immune to another paralytic attack . . . the experiment would be as safe as it could possibly be."

In April 1955, first and second graders were given the newly approved Salk vaccine.

The experiment was not only safe, it was a total success. When blood samples were taken a few weeks after injection with the vaccine, the antibody level in every subject showed a significant increase. Salk was ready to move on to the next trial. But this time, the subjects he would vaccinate had never had polio. This experiment, which was also conducted in secrecy, was riskier than the first, for it was possible the subjects could contract polio from the injection.

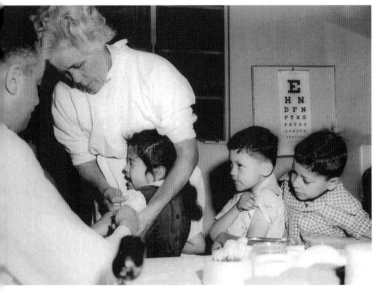

Fortunately, the second trial was also an unqualified success. The subjects' antibody levels rose, indicating that they had developed immunity to the poliovirus, but none of them contracted the disease. After these results, Salk knew that "it was time to move toward more extensive tests. To do this we needed the support of the polio-research community." After some initial debate

THE BATTLE AGAINST POLIO

about the safety of the Salk vaccine, additional trials using a few hundred subjects at a time were done throughout 1953. When each trial produced the same positive results, Salk and his colleagues became increasingly optimistic.

In the summer of 1954, the NFIP sponsored a nationwide vaccination program using Salk's vaccine. It spent approximately $9 million for 27 million doses of the vaccine. Nearly two million children between the ages of six and nine—nicknamed the Polio Pioneers—took part in the program. Half were given the vaccine while the other half, the control group, were given a placebo. Then the country waited for the results.

On April 12, 1955, people heard the announcement they had so long hoped for: "The new Salk vaccine works, is safe, effective and potent." Salk was hailed as a hero by the public and was granted a license to market his vaccine by the government. Doctors across the country and the world could now administer the vaccine to their patients.

Unfortunately, the story of the Salk vaccine has a stain. In April 1955, Cutter Laboratories in California generated a batch of vaccine that mistakenly contained some live viruses. As a result, 204 children contracted polio. Of those children, 153 became paralyzed and 11 died. Some of the victims had not even been the ones to receive the vaccine. They became infected when they associated with those who had been vaccinated—proof that the vaccine had contained live, and therefore contagious, viruses.

This incident, while tragic, did not stop the production or use of the Salk vaccine. Rather, it served as a warning to other man-

The triumph and the tragedy: the Salk vaccine came too late for this man.

Minutes after the success of the Salk vaccine was announced, its manufacturer began to airlift the drug across the United States.

ufacturers to use the utmost care. The effectiveness of the vaccine became apparent within five years. In 1960, the number of polio cases in the United States dropped to 3,190. In 1961, it was down to 1,312. The year 1962 recorded only 910 in the country.

Yet not everybody agreed that the Salk vaccine was the best. Some pointed to the Cutter Laboratories incident as proof that using a killed strain of the virus could be dangerous, since, they argued, there was no way of knowing whether all the viruses had been killed. One person who raised his voice in loud opposition to Salk was Dr. Albert Sabin.

THE SABIN VACCINE

Dr. Albert Sabin was born in Poland. He and his family were Jewish, and in 1921 they moved to the United States to escape persecution. After attending medical school in New York City, Sabin embarked on a prestigious research career studying viruses and working on vaccines. In 1939, he became an associate professor of pediatrics in the College of Medicine of the University of Cincinnati.

During World War II, Sabin served in the Army Medical Corps, working on vaccines for three viral illnesses that plagued the army: hepatitis, dengue fever, and Japanese encephalitis. Experiments were done using both killed and attenuated, or weakened, strains of the viruses that caused these diseases. Sabin's experiences during the war years cemented his belief that live virus vaccines were better than those that used killed viruses.

Although Sabin dealt with a wide variety of viruses, his main interest was poliovirus. When evidence showed that poliovirus entered the body through the mouth, Sabin became convinced that an oral vaccine rather than an injected one would prove to be more effective in preventing the disease. In early 1952, he began work on an attenuated oral vaccine.

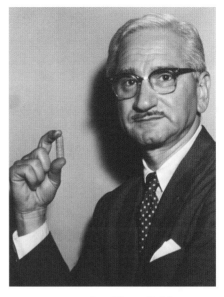

Sabin received little support from the polio community in the United States. In 1953, when Salk was ready to begin small trials with his vaccine, Sabin's vaccine was still in the earliest stages of development. The NFIP threw its weight behind the leader in the race. And when Salk's vaccine proved effective, support for Sabin shrank even more. So Sabin took his experiments abroad, where the Salk vaccine had yet to make an impact.

Dr. Albert Sabin holds a vial of his oral polio vaccine.

By 1955, the oral vaccine was ready for testing. For the next two years, small groups of subjects, including volunteers from prisons, received the Sabin vaccine. The tests turned in positive results, yet the NFIP continued to overlook Sabin and his vaccine. In the end, it was the World Health Organization (WHO) that took on his cause. In 1957, WHO authorized the mass vaccination of children living in areas suffering from polio epidemics, including parts of Russia. By 1959, nearly 4.5 million people in Russia had received the oral vaccine. The incidence of polio in that country decreased markedly between 1957 and 1959.

In the face of such results, the United States finally acknowledged that Sabin's vaccine was as effective as Salk's. In 1960, the Sabin vaccine was licensed for use. In time, the convenience of Sabin's oral vaccine made it more popular than Salk's injection. By 1965, most doctors in the United States and around the world were using the oral vaccine.

The effectiveness of both the Salk and Sabin vaccines was undeniable. The annual average incidence of polio in the United

States decreased from more than 37,000 cases in the years 1951–1955 to fewer than 600 a mere decade later. The last recorded case of "wild" polio—polio contracted naturally through the environment—in the United States occurred in 1979. And in 1991, a Peruvian boy contracted the last known case of wild polio in the Western Hemisphere.

Yet the merits of the Salk versus the Sabin vaccine continue to be debated to this day. In 1997, the Centers for Disease Control (CDC) in Atlanta, Georgia, recognized that the Sabin-type vaccine, known as OPV (oral poliovirus vaccine), had been responsible for causing vaccine-associated paralytic polio in one out of every 2.2 million–3.5 million people. In 1999, the CDC recommended the disuse of the Sabin vaccine in favor of the Salk type.

This recommendation still stands today, but only for citizens of countries where wild polio has been eradicated, such as the United States. In countries where wild polio still causes the disease—Afghanistan, Pakistan, and India, to name three—OPV is the preferred vaccine. This is because OPV both creates antibodies in the blood and blocks the virus from replicating in the intestines. Salk's vaccine, because it is injected into the bloodstream rather than introduced into the digestive system, does not offer this same protection. Therefore, Sabin's oral vaccine is preferred for use in areas where the wild poliovirus is most likely to be ingested.

Regardless of which vaccine children are given, one thing remains certain: thanks to Salk and Sabin, the dreadful crippler has nearly been eradicated from the world.

POLIO TODAY

 olio still exists today, but its sphere of infection has decreased greatly thanks to the Global Polio Eradication Initiative, a joint venture of the World Health Organization, the Centers for Disease Control, UNICEF, and Rotary International. This program was introduced in 1988. That year, approximately 350,000 polio cases were reported worldwide. Within fifteen years, thanks to ongoing mass immunization programs in at-risk countries, that number dropped to less than 700. While polio has yet to be eradicated completely, the disease is definitely dying out.

Yet even if no new cases occur, polio will not truly be gone, for it lives on in the crippled limbs and memories of survivors. It

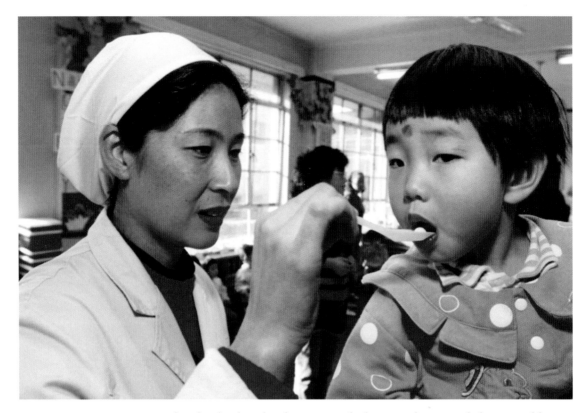

China 1955:
a kindergartner
receives the oral
vaccine. In only a
few short days that
year, China carried
out the largest anti-
polio campaign in
history—more than
80 million children
were immunized.

exists in the books these people have written and the taped inter-
views they've given. It remains as countless photographs of
patients and in the images of the "poster children" for the March
of Dimes. It will be a long time—if ever—before this dread disease
is forgotten.

TIME LINE OF POLIO EVENTS

ca. 1500 B.C. An Egyptian stele of an apparent polio victim is carved

1789: Dr. Michael Underwood writes the first clinical description of polio

1813: Italian surgeon Giovanni Battista Monteggia publishes a much more complete description of poliomyelitis

1840: Dr. Jacob von Heine conducts the first systematic investigation of polio

1870: Dr. Jean-Martin Charcot confirms Heine's theory that polio afflicts the spinal cord

1887: Polio epidemic in Stockholm infects 44 people; Karl Oskar Medin conducts an in-depth study of the disease

1894: Epidemic in Rutland, Vermont, afflicts 132 people

1905: Dr. Ivar Wickman investigates Swedish epidemic and concludes that mild cases of polio are more prevalent than severe cases and are just as capable of spreading the disease

1908: Karl Landsteiner and Erwin Popper prove that a virus causes polio

1916: New York epidemic; 27,000 people in the United States are infected, 7,000 die

1921: Franklin Delano Roosevelt contracts polio

1927: Philip Drinker designs the iron lung

1931: New York City epidemic; Dr. Albert Sabin publishes his first study of poliovirus

1935: Boston epidemic; Annapolis, Maryland: entire city quarantined; President Roosevelt calls off the National Boy Scout Jamboree

1938: National Foundation for Infantile Paralysis (later known as the March of Dimes) is established by FDR

1940s: Australian Sister Elizabeth Kenny moves to the United States, where she revolutionizes the treatment of polio patients

1946: Epidemic leaves 25,000 stricken

1948: John Enders, Thomas Weller, and Frederick Robbins grow poliovirus in cultures, using monkey kidney tissues

1949: Scientists discover the three different types of poliovirus

1952: Polio epidemic in the United States afflicts 57,879—a record high

1955: Jonas Salk's vaccine is pronounced effective and safe and is licensed for marketing

1957: First year the Salk vaccine is widely used; 5,000 polio cases reported

1960: Albert Sabin's vaccine is licensed for marketing

1979: The last case of wild polio in the United States is recorded

1988: WHO and other organizations begin a worldwide campaign to eradicate polio

1991: Last case of wild polio in the Western Hemisphere is recorded

2001: Number of polio cases worldwide is 453

2002: Number of polio cases worlwide climbs to 1,920, due to an epidemic in India

2003: 677 polio cases are reported worldwide

GLOSSARY

anterior horn tissue the part of the spinal cord that contains motor neurons

antibodies agents that attach themselves to viruses and make it impossible for them to enter cells

asymptomatic showing no signs of infection

atrophy weakness from lack of use

attenuated weakened, reduced in the ability to cause harm

autopsy the systematic dissection and analysis of a dead body, performed in order to figure out how and why death occurred

bacteriology the study of bacteria

culture to grow viruses or bacteria in laboratory conditions; material that is grown in this way

dissemination the act of spreading or scattering

electron microscope a sophisticated device that uses electrons, the smallest part of the atom, to help magnify objects too small to see with a light microscope

epidemic an outbreak of a disease that spreads rapidly in a short period of time, affecting a great proportion of a population in a localized geographic area

epidemiologists scientists who study how diseases spread

feces solid waste expelled from the body

formalin a diluted form of the chemical solution formaldehyde, used to deactivate poliovirus to create a killed-virus polio vaccine

hydrotherapy physical therapy performed while immersed in water

immunity natural or induced resistance to infection

interferon a protein generated by cells that have been invaded by a virus; the protein inhibits the replication of the virus in other cells

lesions abnormal changes or marks on bodily tissue indicating injury or disease

microbe an organism of microscopic size or smaller

motor neurons the cells responsible for telling muscles how and when to move

orthopedist a doctor who treats injuries to and illnesses of the bones and muscles

paralysis the inability to move

placebo an inactive preparation given instead of a vaccine or medicine in a controlled experiment to test the effectiveness of the vaccine or medicine

postulates basic principles or requirements

quadriplegic unable to move from the neck down, due to illness or physical trauma that affects the central nervous system

quarantine the isolation of individuals infected with a contagious disease to prevent them from passing the infection on to others

spasms uncontrolled, involuntary contractions of muscles

spinal meningitis a bacterial infection that causes inflammation of the membranes surrounding the spinal cord; can be fatal in infants and young children

vaccination the administration of a vaccine

vaccine solutions containing either live, weakened viruses or killed viruses that are injected into the bloodstream or administered orally in order to stimulate the immune system into making antibodies

virus a submicroscopic parasite composed of a protein shell surrounding genetic material that invades a host in order to reproduce

TO FIND OUT MORE

BOOKS

Bredeson, Carmen. *Jonas Salk: People to Know*. Hillside, NJ: Enslow Publishers, 1993.
An informative biography written for the middle-grade reader.

Crofford, Emily. *Healing Warrior: A Story about Sister Elizabeth Kenny*. Minneapolis: Carolrhoda Books, 1989.
Tells the story of the woman who revolutionized treatments for polio sufferers. For the middle-grade audience.

Draper, Allison Stark. *Polio: Epidemics Deadly Diseases Throughout History*. New York: Rosen Publishing Group, 2001.
A comprehensive yet easy-to-read overview of the history of

polio, including the present state of the disease.

Kehret, Peg. *Small Steps: The Year I Got Polio*. Morton Grove, IL: Albert Whitman, 1996.

Written for the middle-grade audience, this autobiography tells of one woman's experiences with polio.

Sherrow, Victoria. *Polio Epidemic: Crippling Virus Outbreak*. Berkeley Heights, NJ: Enslow Publishers, 2001.

An overview of the disease, written for the middle grades.

Silverstein, Alvin, Virginia Silverstein, and Laura Silverstein Nunn. *Polio*. Berkeley Heights, NJ: Enslow Publishers, 2001.

An in-depth look at polio, the people who fought against it, and the present state of the disease.

ON THE INTERNET*

www.cdc.gov

Official Web site of the Centers for Disease Control; includes a PDF file with descriptions of polio symptoms, the poliovirus, vaccines, and a brief history of the disease.

www.fdrlibrary.marist.edu/

This online library gives access to information on and papers by Franklin D. Roosevelt. Included are articles about FDR's fund-raising efforts for the March of Dimes.

www.bluelf.com

Includes a polio patient's memories of growing up with polio, as well as information on the disease.

www.marchofdimes.com

Official Web site of the organization; includes history of the March of Dimes and information on polio, polio eradication, and post-polio syndrome.

www.feri.org

Official Web site of the Franklin and Eleanor Roosevelt Institute; includes archives of some of FDR's speeches as well as an overview of his polio history.

www.pbs.org/wgbh/aso/ontheedge/polio

Comic book-style look at the development of the Salk vaccine and the history of polio, aimed at middle graders.

www.polio-vaccine.com

Provides time line of polio events from 1580 B.C. to present day.

www.polioeradication.org

Official site of the Global Polio Eradication Initiative; includes up-to-date information on polio in the world today.

*All Internet sites were available and accurate when this book was sent to press.

BIBLIOGRAPHY

Black, Kathryn. *In the Shadow of Polio: A Personal and Social History.* Reading, MA: Addison-Wesley, 1996.

Brown, David. "Study Challenges FDR's Polio." *Washington Post,* October 31, 2003.

Brown, James Gary. *My Experience with Polio.* 1999. www.bluelf.com

Cohn, Victor. *Sister Kenny: The Woman Who Challenged the Doctors.* Minneapolis: University of Minnesota Press, 1975.

Gallagher, Hugh Gregory. *FDR's Splendid Deception.* Arlington, VA: Vandamere Press, 1999.

Gould, Tony. *A Summer Plague: Polio and Its Survivors.* New Haven: Yale University Press, 1995.

Halstead, Laura S. *Managing Post-Polio.* Arlington, VA: ABI Professional Publications, 1998.

Hoff, Brent, and Carter Smith III. *Mapping Epidemics: A Historical Atlas of Disease.* New York: Franklin Watts, 2000.

Kehret, Peg. *Small Steps: The Year I Got Polio.* Morton Grove, IL: Albert Whitman, 1996.

Kenny, Sister Elizabeth. *And They Shall Walk.* New York: Dodd, Mead & Company, 1944.

Paul, John R. *A History of Poliomyelitis.* New Haven: Yale University Press, 1971.

Roosevelt, Franklin D. *Radio Address on a Program of Assistance for the Crippled,* 1931. www.feri.org/archives

Sass, Edmond. *Polio's Legacy: An Oral History.* Lanham, MD: University Press of America, 1996.

——. *Remembering Polio: A Ghost from Summers Past.*
www.employees.csbsju.edu./esass/remembering polio.htm

Seavey, Nina Gilden, Jane S. Smith, and Paul Wagner. *A Paralyzing Fear: The Triumph of Polio in America.* New York: TV Books, 1998.

Sherrow, Victoria. *Polio Epidemic: Crippling Virus Outbreak.* Berkeley Heights, NJ: Enslow Publishers, 2001.

Smith, Jane S. *Patenting the Sun: Polio and the Salk Vaccine.* New York: William Morrow, 1990.

NOTES ON QUOTATIONS

The quotations in this book are from the following sources:

Chapter One: From Obscurity to Epidemic

p. 1 "I woke up," Sass, *Polio's Legacy,* p. 30.

p. 3: "I was sitting," Brown, *My Experience with Polio.*

p. 9: "debility of the lower extremities," Paul, *A History of Poliomyelitis,* p. 22.

p. 9: "usually attacks children," Ibid., p. 22.

p. 9: "Nothing has seemed," Ibid., pp. 22–23.

p. 9: "it [the paralysis] begins," Ibid., p. 28.

p. 9: "point[ed] to an affection," Ibid., p. 32.

Chapter Two: The Early Years of Polio Research

p. 13: "One night, I have been told," Gould, *A Summer Plague,* p. 10.

p. 13: "light and unimportant form," Paul, *A History of Poliomyelitis,* p. 73.

p. 15: "an acute nervous disease," Ibid., p. 80.

p. 20: "New York. March 9," Ibid., p. 116.

Chapter Three: Polio on the Rise

p. 22: "Being crippled," Roosevelt, *Radio Address on a Program of Assistance for the Crippled.*

p. 27: "The poisonous gases," Gould, *A Summer Plague,* p. 20.

p. 28: "First symptoms," Gallagher, *FDR's Splendid Deception,*
    pp.10–11.

p. 29: "Father was unbelievably," Ibid., p. 16.

p. 30: "I can't tell you," Brown, "Study Challenges FDR's Polio."

p. 31: "The legs are really improving," Gallagher, *FDR's Splendid
    Deception,* p. 36.

p. 33: "For some years," Gould, *A Summer Plague,* p. 120.

Chapter Four: Coping with the Incurable

p. 35: "As I stood," Kenny, *And They Shall Walk,* p. 204.

p. 39: "I want them," Ibid., p. 24.

p. 39: "the extraordinary attitude," Ibid., p. 92.

p. 39: "how many promising," Ibid., p. 92.

p. 40: "I was informed," Ibid., pp. 267 and 268.

p. 41: "I was pushed," Kehret, *Small Steps,* p. 54.

p. 41: "I was kept," Sass, *Remembering Polio.*

p. 43: "I had body wedging," Brown, *My Experience with Polio.*

Chapter Five: Vaccine Trials—and Errors

p. 44: "The fight against," Paul, *A History of Poliomyelitis,* p. 319.

p. 45: "no harmful effects," Ibid., p. 255.

p. 46: "It looks as though," and "Gentlemen, this is one time,"Gould,
    A Summer Plague, p. 68.

p. 50: "There were sixteen," Sherrow, *Polio Epidemic,* p. 18.

p. 50: "I can remember," Seavey, *A Paralyzing Fear,* p. 254.

p. 50: "I do remember seeing," Ibid., p. 78.

Chapter Six: Salk and Sabin

p. 53: "When you give," Seavey, *A Paralyzing Fear,* p. 183.

p. 54: "take blood," and "since the subjects," Gould, *A Summer
    Plague,* p. 132.

p. 54: "it was time," Ibid., p. 133.

p. 55: "The new Salk vaccine," Sherrow, *Polio Epidemic,* p. 36.

INDEX

Page numbers for illustrations are in boldface

abortive polio, 4
adults crippled by polio, viii, 6, 7, 8, **8**, 12, 28-33, **31**, **55**
American Epidemiological Society, 33
American Public Health Association, 46
animals
  extermination of, 26, **26**
  in scientific experiments, 18-19, **19**, 21, 54
antibodies, 7-8
atrophy, 5
Australia, polio treatments in, 38-39, **39**

Boyer, Carol, 50-51
Brodie, Maurice, 45-46, 47
Brown, James Gary, 3, 43
Bull, A. C., 14

Caverly, Charles, 15
Centers for Disease Control (CDC), 58, 59
Charcot, Jean-Martin, 9-10
China, anti-polio campaign in, **60**
Cutter Laboratories, 55, 56

Drinker, Philip, 36
D.T. Watson Home for Crippled Children, PA, 54

Enders, John, 47, **47**, 53
epidemics, polio, 13-16, 22-28, **23**, **24**, **25**, **26**, **27**, 29, 35-36, 49-51, **49**, **51**

Flexner, Simon, 19-21, **20**, 33
formalin, 53
fund-raising for polio, 49, **49**

Georgia Warm Springs Foundation, 32
Global Polio Eradication Initiative, 59
Goldman, Armond, 30
Guillain-Barré syndrome, 30

Heine, Jacob von, 6, 9, 10, 15, **16**

immunity, polio, 7-8
inapparent polio, 4, 7
Industrial Revolution, 10-12, **11**, **12**
infantile paralysis, 4, 15
insects, 26-27, **27**
interferon, 7
iron lungs, **34**, 36-38, **37**, 50-51, **51**

Jenner, Edward, 44

Kehret, Peg Schulze, 1-2, 41
Kenny Method therapy, 39, 40-41, 42, 43
Kenny, Sister Elizabeth, 35, 38-41, **39**, **41**, 44
Koch, Robert, 17
Koch's postulates, 17, 19
Kolmer, John A., 45-46

Kussmaul, Adolph, 6

Landsteiner, Karl J., **16**, 17-19, **17**
Lovett, Robert W., 29

McDonnell, Aeneas, 38
March of Dimes, 33, 49, 60
Medin, Karl Oskar, 14-15, **16**
microbes, 17
Mitchell, John P., 25
Monteggia, Giovanni Battista, 9

National Foundation for Infantile
     Paralysis (NFIP), 32-33, 37,
     40, 44, 48, 55, 57
neurons, 5, 6, 7
New York City Epidemic, 1916,
     23-28, **23**, **24**, **25**, **26**, **27**, 29
Nobel Prize, 17, 47
non-paralytic polio, 4

O'Connor, Basil, 48
Olympic Games, 42
Owen, Dick, 40, 43

paralytic polio, 4-5, **4**
pathogens, 17
Polio Pioneers, 55
poliomyelitis (polio), ix, **x**, 1-2
   early history of, 8-10, **8**, **9**
   early years of polio research,
      13-21, **14**, **16**, **17**, **19**, **20**
   and the Industrial Revolution,
      10-12, **11**, **12**
   last recorded cases of, 58
   names for, 4, 6, 15

New York City Epidemic,
   1916, 23-28 **23**, **24**, **25**, **26**,
   27, 29
1952 Epidemic, 49-51, **49**, **51**
polio today, 59-60, **60**
polio vaccines, 6, 8, 21, 44-51, **47**,
   52, 53-58 **54**, **55**, **56**, **57**, **60**
time line of polio events, 61
treatment of, **34**, 35-43, **37**,
   39, **41**, **42**
what is, 2-5, **3**, **5**, 7-8
wild polio, 58
poliovirus, 2-4, **3**, 5, 7-8, 12
   discovery in digestive tract, 33
   discovery of, 17-19, **19**
   three poliovirus types, 6, **6**, 7,
      8, 46, 48
   Typing Program, 48-49
Popper, Erwin, 17-19

quarantine, 25, 26

rabies, 26
respirator centers, 37, **37**
Robbins, Frederick, 47, 53
Rockefeller Institute, 20, 21
Roosevelt, Eleanor, 28, 29, 31
Roosevelt, Franklin Delano, viii, 22,
   28-33, **30**, **31**, 37-38, 40, 44
Roosevelt, James, 29
Rotary International, 59
Rudolph, Wilma, 42, **42**

Sabin, Albert, 56-58, **57**
Salk, Jonas, 48, **52**, 53-56, **54**,
   55, **56**, 57-58

Scandinavia, polio outbreaks in, 13-16
Schwartz, Arvid, 50
Science, 47
Scott, Sir Walter, 13, **14**
Sister Elizabeth Kenny Institute, 40
summer of 1952, polio epidemic during, 49-51, **49**

Temple, Ed, 42
Toronto splints, 41, 43
Typing Program, 48-49

Underwood, Michael, 6, 9
UNICEF, 59

vaccines, polio
  injected vaccine, 6, 8, 21, 44-51, **47**, **52**, 53-56, **54**, **55**, **56**, 58
  oral vaccine, 56-58, **57**, **60**

Warm Springs, Georgia, 31-32
waterborne disease, polio as a, 3, 11-12, **12**
Weaver, Harry, 48
Weller, Thomas, 47, 53
white blood cells, 7
Wickman, Ivar, 6, 15-16, **16**
wild polio, 58
Wilson, James L., 37
World Health Organization (WHO), 57, 59
World War II, 39-40, 56

yellow fever, 26-27

ABOUT THE AUTHOR

Stephanie True Peters grew up in Westborough, Massachusetts. After graduating with a degree in history from Bates College, she moved to Boston, where she worked as an editor of children's books. She made the jump from editor to writer soon after the birth of her son. Since then, she has authored a number of non-fiction books for young people, including the other titles in the Epidemic! series. Stephanie lives in Mansfield, Massachusetts, with her husband, Dan, and their two children, Jackson and Chloe. She enjoys going on adventures with her family, beachcombing on Cape Cod, and teaching kick-boxing classes at the local YMCA.